Teaching
About
Phonics

Teaching About Phonics

ALBERT J. MAZURKIEWICZ

Kean College of New Jersey

ST. MARTIN'S PRESS
NEW YORK

Preface

Nothing is more basic in education than skill in reading; yet evidence continues to accumulate to show that untold numbers of children fail badly in their efforts to master the process. One of the most important and basic causes of failure is the difficulty a child faces in decoding print to speech and meaning since it has been shown that printed English is a complex of inconsistency. A welter of research about the symbol-to-sound correspondences of the language has accumulated in a diverse number of journals and texts, but it has largely been ignored. That research, if pulled together into one source, can be shown to be of high significance in correcting long-standing errors in instruction and in developing effective instructional strategies to reduce the child's chances for failure while promoting increased understanding of how the printed form of our language works. This book is the result of my efforts to meet that challenge and long-standing need. Additional research, not hitherto available to fill in the informational base, was conducted expressly for this volume. It produced fresh insights on the basic correspondences of sounds to symbols used in decoding print, and it resulted in the construction of generalizations to provide a new basis for examining supposed inconsistencies and to strengthen instruction in decoding. For the first time, decoding skills are related to the frequency of occurrences of spelling-to-sound correspondences; instructional procedures are developed from research evidence rather than from opinion.

The book is directed at the pre-service undergraduate and the in-service graduate student who must possess basic knowledge of how the orthography of American English is structured as he or she pursues the requisite skills for teaching competence in reading. It should serve as a basic text in beginning courses such as teaching reading in the elementary school or in early childhood, as well as in graduate courses in these same areas. It can serve as an invaluable source book for the specialist-in-training or in-service whose informational base about the language is weak or in error.

The book is directed at the in-service teacher as well because he or she most often indicates gaps in information, notes that insufficient time was devoted to this area in courses taken at college, often admits confusion in sorting out the claims of writers, and has little time to read across the research literature to develop a comprehensive understanding. Since the in-service teacher is often the only source to whom the child can turn when attempting to succeed in reading, the teacher particularly needs the information embodied in this text to edit incorrect or misstated materials in workbooks and guides and to provide correct, detailed information to help the child succeed.

Although it is designed to be of specific benefit to teachers and specialists in reading, the content of this book, particularly of Chapters 2, 3, and 4, should prove useful as well to students struggling to learn English as a second language via print.

Chapter 1 contains a brief introduction to characterize the child as an illiterate and as a reader, and relates the child's development in reading to stages in his or her cognitive development. Chapter 2 considers the significant sounds of speech as they relate to American English and as necessary to clarify meanings of terms common to instruction. Chapters 3 and 4 provide a wealth of detail on the print correspondences of consonants (the backbone of language) and vowels (the pure music of speech). In these chapters, 112 consonant and vowel spellings are isolated for instruction using generalizations, grapheme bases, and associational activity. Chapter 5 points up the research base for recommended instructional activities, while emphasizing practical, detailed, instructional procedure.

The reader is encouraged to return to and retake the pretest,

"What Do You Know About Phonics?" which begins this volume, on completing a reading of its contents. The pretest should prove a valuable means of demonstrating what the reader has learned, as well as how much error or lack of knowledge he or she originally possessed. It should serve as a valuable corrective device in promoting effective instruction in reading.

Contents

"What Do You Know About Phonics?"

Judging by the responses of a wide sample of students, teachers, and specialists to this question in a recent study (Mazurkiewicz, 1975), the answer would most likely be "nothing," "little," "a great deal," or "not as much as I should." Before you delve into this text, you can sample the information it will supply and evaluate your current knowledge of the English language by taking the short quiz below. As with any pretest, the results will help you to understand your strengths and weaknesses and to establish a basis for improving your understanding of the phonics of English.

Directions: Answer each multiple-choice question by circling the correct answer; when the question requests information, write the answer on the blank line. Don't neglect to answer a question because you think the answer is obvious.

1. The alphabet we use to represent English speech is called the
   a. English alphabet   b. Roman alphabet
   c. Graeco-Roman alphabet   d. Indo-European alphabet
2. How many letters in the twenty-six-letter alphabet we use represent *vowel* sounds only?
   1   2   3   4   5   6   7
3. What letters of the alphabet represent vowel sounds only?
   _____
4. How many letters in the alphabet represent *consonant* sounds only?
   18   19   20   22   23
5. How many letters represent both consonant and vowel sounds?
   _____
6. How many significant sounds are there in English speech?
   _____
7. How many significant vowel sounds are there in the English language? _____
8. Which letter of the alphabet sometimes represents a single consonant sound, but most often represents four different pairs of two consonant sounds? _____
9. How many different sounds does the letter *s* represent? _____

Circle all letters, words, or spelling patterns in each row that illustrate the word preceding the row.

10. consonant   *r j k y m u t i z p*
11. vowel   *a h b y l w o e v u*
12. long vowel   *rate tie rule now road seed*
13. diphthong   *noise I how utility out shoe*
14. digraph   *them church seem phone pick flew*
15. blend   *th ph cl rt an dr sp*

In teaching reading, the following generalizations are often used. Indicate whether you do or would use the generalization when the occasion arose in the classroom. Differences in the way you might state the generalization should be disregarded if the essential information is contained in the sentence.

16. Vowels in open syllables (such as the first vowel in *lady* or *baby*) are usually long.   Yes   No

17. The *e* at the end of words (such as *since, give, turtle, toe, came*) is usually silent and indicates that the first vowel usually says its own name.   Yes   No
18. When there are two vowels together in a word, the first is usually long and the second silent.   Yes   No

Now check your answers with those found on page xiv.

REFERENCE

Mazurkiewicz, Albert J. "What Do Teachers Know About Phonics." *Reading World* 14 (March 1975): 165 – 177.

ANSWERS

1. Roman alphabet
2. 1 or 3 (See page 32)
3. *a* (See page 32)
4. 18 (See page 32)
5. 5 or 7 (See page 32)
6. Any number from 39 to 44 (See page 20)
7. 8, 11, or 15 (See pages 9, 16, 20)
8. *x*
9. 4 (See page 32)
10. All letters should have been circled (See page 32)
11. *a, h, y, w, o, e, u* (See page 32)
12. *rate, road,* and *seed*—the others are generally considered to be diphthongs (See page 15)
13. all but *shoe,* or all the words should have been circled (See page 15)
14. *them, seem, phone, pick* (*ch* and *fl* represent two sounds) (See page 139)
15. *cl, rt, an, dr, sp* (only these are blends, but *cl, dr,* and *sp* are usually given special instructional attention) (See page 139)
16. No (See page 82)
17. Yes and No (See page 108)
18. No (See page 107)

Count number 17 correct if you said yes. Assign five points to each question. Your total score, evaluated according to the following chart, indicates your "phonics IQ":

85 – 90   Genius: You should be in a college or university teaching teachers.
70 – 80   Superior: You qualify as a budding specialist but should review this book.
45 – 65   Average: This book will help eliminate confusion and provide the knowledge you need.
0 – 40   Below average: Don't give up. This book will be of great value to you.

Teaching
About
Phonics

1

Introduction

The words *rate, call, for, not, hour,* and *boy* illustrate a basic concept in reading English that is largely passed over in teaching reading: that the beginner at any age level must read not only from left to right but also from right to left to decode words. And adults, when confronted with an unfamiliar word, must do this as well. Reading a letter in an English word is not a simple task of decoding grapheme-phoneme correspondences in a left-to-right sequence but is in fact dependent on examining the surrounding letters. The vowel letter *a* represents one sound in *rat*, changes to another sound in *rate*, and is modified to a third in *call*. In each case, the environment of consonants alters the pronunciation of *a*. Reading *rat* becomes a sequential pattern of decoding 1-2-3, whereas *rate* becomes 1-2-3-4-2-3 or 1-2-4-2-3, and *call*, 1-2-3-2-3. Letter patterns such as *ph, sh, th, ai, ay, ce, ca, ge,* or *go* with which we represent the sounds of English enable us to decode a word; however, for most of these, there are pronunciation exceptions. For instance, *ai* is pronounced one way in *paid* and another way in *said; ge* in *get* is different from *ge* in *gem.*

Learning to decode written English is a complicated task, yet

3

hundreds of thousands succeed each year in mastering it. However, whereas mature adult readers by-pass the stage of decoding by letter-sound and letter-sound environments, beginning readers have no real alternatives available to them, and even in controlled and reformed orthographies they must learn these correspondences in order to master the more efficient procedures used by adults. Learning to read English in the acquisition stage is primarily a process of learning to decode by learning up to 211 distinct letter-sound correspondences, 166 rules (60 of which relate to consonants), 45 exceptions to rules (which are rules in themselves), and 69 spelling-pattern rules. These figures are based on an analysis by Berdiansky, Cronnell, and Koehler (1968) of 6,092 one- and two-syllable words among 9,000 different words contained in the oral and written vocabularies of six- to nine-year-old children. In the time since that analysis was done, additional research has established that this quite exceptional burden placed upon beginning readers may be modified and reduced. It is the intent of this text to set out those procedures to reduce the burden.

Phonics sometimes provides only an approximation of the sound that a letter or spelling pattern represents. When a word is familiar, children, often without additional help, will jump from this kind of approximation to the correct pronunciation. When a word is not in children's acoustic store, they will, in reading silently, respond to that approximation, which is a primitive or partial auditory label, until called upon to read orally, at which point the pronunciation will be corrected for them. Frequently, children will mispronounce a word in speech after having met it in print first and having attached an approximation of the correct pronunciation to it on the basis of the rules of correspondence. Mature readers behave similarly, often not bothering to pronounce an unfamiliar word that they encounter in print initially. Teachers of reading should expect no more of children than they do of mature, skillful readers. Furthermore, they should recognize the limitations of phonic instruction to produce accurate sound correspondences for English, keeping in mind that dialect differences must modify general rules of pronunciation of words, and that mature reading of English is produced developmentally through an interaction of learned skills with printed materials over a period of time.

Jean Piaget (1967) provides a number of useful ideas concerning the developing child. One of Piaget's concepts relates to the child's perceptual abilities at different ages. Piaget has noted, for example, that at about age three the child centers his or her perception on the figure in a given ground (for our purposes, *figure* can be taken to mean a word; and *ground,* the page on which the word appears), but that by age eight-and-a-half the child decenters to the ground, that is, has a flexibility in procedure for examining words. This suggests that at age three the child usually focuses on individual letters or some internal aspect of a word, but that by age eight-and-a-half he or she can use the letters and the configuration (the outline or shape of the word) as well as other aspects of a word to identify it. Research has tended to confirm the existence of perceptual decentration in children.

If this theory is applied to a reading program, the program should not exclude sight vocabulary (words taught as wholes). The reason behind this is that a child might use some internal aspects of a word in recognizing it. Thus, it is desirable to include the letter and its features as well as a symbol-to-sound correspondence in a beginning program. Furthermore, a child of eight or nine is capable of using clues other than the letter, and, like an adult, when he or she has learned to read, reads with minimum cues, recognizing words using only part of the total information a word contains, such as the upper half of the word, two or three letters of a word, and so on. We know too, from the late nineteenth- and early twentieth-century work of Javal (1968) and Messmer (1903) that the fixation point in reading is between the middle and top of lower-case letters and that the upper half of letters carries most of their relevant identifying features. A child who reads at an average rate of fifty to sixty words per minute at age nine is incapable of attending to all the individual letters in these words; what the child is, in fact, doing is using the context, his familiarity with language, as well as the cue value of the upper half (the coastline) of words to recognize and assimilate them.

At the outset of reading instruction, most children are "illiterate," although in the years before they enter school they have usually had multiple opportunities to examine print, as for example, in their home environment or on television. For the vast majority of children, literacy training, or instruction in reading, is formalized in the school years. Through repeated exposure to print and the necessity of applying information they have learned to analyzing print, children develop their skill in decoding, and in this way they move away from a letter-by-letter or a group-of-letters analysis to a rapid recognition of words using fewer and fewer cues.

The relatively short-term objectives of a primary reading program must take cognizance of the developing child's abilities as outlined above and provide a systematic program to help the child master the requisite skills and abilities necessary to achieve minimum-cue-based reading.

REFERENCES

Berdiansky, Betty, Cronnell, Bruce, and Koehler, John. *Spelling-Sound Relations and Primary Form-Class Descriptions for Speech-Comprehension Vocabularies of 6–9 Year Olds.* Southwest Regional Laboratory for Educational Research and Development, Technical Report no. 15, 1968.

Javal, Emile. Reported in Edmund B. Huey, *The Psychology and Pedagogy of Reading.* Cambridge, Mass.: MIT Press, 1968.

Messmer, Oskar. "Zur Psychologie des Lesens bei Kinder und Erwashsemen." *Archiv fur Gesamte Psychologie* (December 1903): 190–298.

Piaget, Jean. Discussed in David Elkind, "Piaget's Theory of Perceptual Development: Its Application to Reading and Special Education." *Journal of Special Education* 1 (1967): 357–361.

2

Phonetics,
Phonemics,
and Phonics

Although voluminous studies have been conducted in an attempt
to understand the difficulties children have in learning to read
written English, it can nonetheless be safely said that reading instruction today is still more of an art than a science. There is little
agreement within the field about basic terminology, the value and
use of generalizations, or the organization of instruction of the body
of spelling patterns representing the phonemes of English. Little
consensus exists as well on what one might consider the most basic
points concerning the reading process: the number and variety of
the English speech-sounds the child possesses. Even the basic
question—How phonetic is English?—is open to dispute. Yet, as
will be seen in the following pages, these disagreements can be resolved. Indeed, they must be if, in fact, we are to eliminate barriers
to reading achievement for the young child.

Although the statement that students of the developing child
recognize that babies of all nationalities babble using the same fifty
or so phonemes of speech and typically have an excellent command

of the structure and syntax of the native language before entering school states a known fact, linguists would argue that the word *phoneme* is used incorrectly in this context. Linguists hold that a phoneme is the smallest semantically functional unit of sound that can be identified in an act of speech. They point out that a phoneme should not be confused with a speech-sound, although it is in fact one. Two speech-sounds, such as the consonant sound at the beginning of *but* and the end of *tub*, may be phonetically different, that is, different in the way they are produced or heard, and still be examples of the same phoneme.

The speech-sounds represented by the letter *p* in the words *pen* and *spend* are phonetically different, the first being aspirated, [p], and the second unaspirated, [p^c]. However, in English these words are never distinguished on the basis of the difference in speech-sounds since this difference is not semantically functional; that is, there is no difference in meaning expressed by this phonetic difference. The two sounds are merely contextual, or environmental, variants of the same phoneme.

Since babies at the stage of babbling are prelinguistic, that is, incapable of using language in a meaningful way, they are not expressing semantically functional speech-sounds and by definition would not be expressing phonemes. Their speech-sounds may be referred to as specific phonemes only when they have become semantically functional units in the developing language code.

Although the phonemes in English are relatively few, most phonemes in this language have more than one contextual variant. Research has demonstrated that no speech-sound is ever repeated in exactly the same way, even when spoken by the same individual. By repeating the words *tub, rabbit*, and *but* to oneself, one can begin to recognize that the absence or presence of a sound before or after the speech-sound /b/ affects the quality or nature of the sound heard or produced. These contextual variations are thought of as a class or family of speech-sounds that we call the phoneme. Whereas some linguists would agree that the phoneme is a class or family of speech-sounds, others hold that it is a bundle of simultaneous acoustical elements called distinctive features. For our purposes, however, the first definition will suffice.

Speech-sounds are usually referred to as phones in linguistic science. Thus, [p] in *pen* and [p^c] in *spend* are individually called *phones*, but collectively the phones [p] and [p^c] are called *allophones*, or different phones, of the phoneme /p/. Phones and allophones are usually placed between brackets [ ], whereas phonemes or combinations thereof are placed between diagonals / /. An allophone of /p/ does not describe or identify the phoneme /p/, but the allophones of /p/ are collectively the family we call the phoneme /p/.

Although linguists disagree on the number of phonemes in the English language, that disagreement has little practical effect for those who teach reading. One linguist, for example, indicates that there are only eight vowel phonemes in the English language, whereas others identify eleven or fifteen. In the first case, the linguist is identifying the simple vowel phonemes as represented in the words *pat, pet, pit, pot, putt, put* and the first vowel phoneme in the words *obey* and *audacious.* The linguist who identifies eleven or fifteen vowel phonemes has added three to seven complex phonemes, or phonemic clusters, which include what are popularly called long vowels and/or diphthongs. For example, the first vowel letter in the word *utility* represents a sound sequence that is made up of two phonemes: the /y/ as in *yo-yo* and /ထ/ as in sh*oe.* Although the letter *u* has generally been called a long vowel, an analysis of the phonemes that this complex vowel contains, /y/ and /ထ/, indicates that it is not a single vowel sound, but rather a group of sounds, and that it might be better referred to as a diphthong or phonemic cluster.

Disagreement among linguists as to the number of phonemes of General American Speech is based largely on theoretical grounds and at times seems to be a matter of preference. Such theoretical disputes need not concern us except as they give rise to estimates of the number of phonemes in American English, which may vary from a low of twenty-eight to a high of fifty-four. Rather, we should note that adult dictionaries generally agree on forty-four phonemes and reformed orthography alphabeticists on forty. Still, these disagreements can be and should be understood.

The six simple vowels of English presented in Chart 1 can be

CHART 1

p*i*t	p*u*t
p*e*t	p*u*tt
p*a*t	p*o*t

extended to include sounds that appear in my *idiolect* (the sounds of one person's speech as contrasted with *dialect*, the sounds of speech peculiar to a group of people in a given region or area) but that might not be distinguished by someone else as essentially different sounds. The sounds represented by the *i* in *children*, the *a* in *about*, and the *o* in *shot*, as seen in Chart 2, are heard and considered

CHART 2

pit	children	put
pet	putt	about
pat	pot	shot

y   w

h

to be semantically different by some linguists and are often listed as the nine simple vowel sounds of speech. These nine vowel sounds do not constitute all the basic sounds of speech, since Chart 2 suggests that *y*, *w*, and *h* also have some relationship to these basic nine sounds. Indeed, the letters *y*, *w*, and *h* are used here to represent the semivowels of the English language. Semivowels are speech-sounds of vowel quality that are ordinarily recognized as consonants. By simple combination of the /i/ in *pit* with the /y/, we can notate a complex vowel sound /iy/, the vowel sound ordinarily heard in *seed*. The combination of the /e/ in *pet* with /y/ would represent the /ey/ sound in *say*. Thus, a thirty-six-vowel sound chart (Chart 3) can be created to show the simple vowels and these vowels

CHART 3

pit	children	put		iy	iy	uy
pet	putt	about		ey	uy	ay
pat	pot	shot		ay	oy	oy

ih	ih	uh
eh	uh	ah
ah	oh	oh

iw	iw	uw
ew	uw	aw
aw	ow	ow

in combination with the semivowels *y*, *h*, and *w*. Although all these vowel sounds do exist, most should be thought of as allophones, or variations of a given phoneme, and of little or no consequence in teaching reading. The letter combinations used in Chart 3 are inadequate to the task of representing and distinguishing between those phonemes, but the thirty-six-vowel system illustrated in this chart does provide graphic evidence for the reasons why linguists disagree about the number of phonemes in English.

THE CONSONANT PHONEMES

Dictionary writers and alphabeticists do generally agree on the number of significant phonemes that need to be symbolized and, more often than not, use diacritic systems to symbolize the significant phonemes of English. These systems, which often vary from one dictionary to another for copyright reasons alone, are frequently supplemented by key words at the bottom of each page. In most cases, readers use the key words, and the diacritic system itself becomes superfluous. Since, for our purposes, we must use some symbol system to identify the significant phonemes of American English, we will thus utilize, compare, and contrast three different systems. Table 1 identifies the twenty-four consonant phonemes common to a phonemic system identified by Betts (1974) for primary-level pupils, an adult notational system (Soffietti, 1968), and Pitman's initial teaching alphabet (1964).

Pitman's initial teaching alphabet (i.t.a.) is the notational system used in this text because it is the simplest and most easily recognizable system when referring to the consonant and vowel phonemes and is not confused by adult readers. For example, the second consonant phoneme in Table 1, represented by *ch* in the phonemic alphabet, can be confused since, in print, *ch* represents three different phonemes, the sounds heard in the words *chew, machine,* and *character.* Although detailed descriptions are given later, it should be noted here that the phoneme /ȼh/, *ch*air, is treated by each system as though it were a single consonant phoneme. For the purpose of teaching children to read, this is the correct approach; the acquisition stage of reading should not be made any more complex than necessary. But dictionaries and linguists identify this as a complex phoneme. In the international phonetic alphabet (IPA), it is identified as /tʃ/; in i.t.a. symbols, it could be written as /tʃh/; and it is identified as a diphthong /difthoŋ/ in such dictionaries as *The Random House Dictionary of American English* (1960) as well as by a host of linguists. Apparently, then, there are both consonant diphthongs and vowel diphthongs, although this distinction is rarely made. Instead, both are simply identified as diphthongs. Since /j/ as used by all three systems is also identified as a diphthong (written /dʒ/ or /dg/), it is desirable that we define the terms.

Diphthong is a Greek word that means having two sounds (di = two, phthongus = sound). The phoneme /b/ could thus be called a phthong; one-sound phonemes could be called monophthongs, and three-sound phonemes could be called triphthongs. Such is the case, of course. The words *fire, our,* and *flower,* having, respectively, one, two, and three significant vowel letters, are examples of words that contain the triphthong. Rewritten in i.t.a., the vowel phonemes in *our* and *flower* would be represented as /ou u/, and in *fire* as /ie u/. In each case, the diphthong is identified by a ligatured symbol.

Using the term *diphthong* to mean a phoneme with two sounds, it should be clear why /ȼh/ and /j/ should be called diphthongs by linguists, and why the term should be qualified when used to describe only certain of the vowel phonemes, for instance, the /ou/ in *out* and the /oi/ in *oil.*

In each of the three notational systems there is a redundancy, and the number of consonants in each list could be reduced by at least two. Since there is a *t* and a ʃh in i.t.a., a *t* and a *sh* in the phonemic alphabet, and a *t* and a š in Soffietti's alphabet, we could eliminate *ch*, č, and ȼh. Similarly, since we have *d* and *zh* in the first, *d* and ž in the second, and *d* and ʒ in the third, all of which combined would represent the diphthong /j/, we could eliminate this character as well. On this basis, the irreducible consonant phoneme system would appear to be composed of twenty-two symbols. However, the question of how many symbols is not significant to those who must

TABLE 1. Consonant Phonemes as Symbolized by Three Systems

	Phonemic	Soffietti	i.t.a.	Key Word
1.	b	b	b	*b*ell
2.	ch	č	ꟳh	*ch*air
3.	d	d	d	*d*og
4.	f	f	f	*f*ish
5.	g	g	g	*g*oat
6.	h	h	h	*h*orse
7.	j	j	j	*j*ack-o-lantern
8.	k	k	k + c	*k*ey + *c*at
9.	l	l	l	*l*ion
10.	m	m	m	*m*onkey
11.	n	n	n	*n*est
12.	ng	ŋ	ꞑ	ri*ng*
13.	p	p	p	*p*encil
14.	r	r	r + ꞧ	*r*abbit + gi*r*l
15.	s	s	s	*S*anta
16.	sh	š	ʃh	*sh*oe
17.	t	t	t	*t*able
18.	th	θ	ꞇh	*th*umb
19.	*th*	ð	ꝺh	fea*th*er
20.	v	v	v	*v*alentine
21.	w	w	w + ꞷh	*w*agon + *wh*istle
22.	y	y	y	*y*o-*y*o
23.	z	z	z + ꙅ	*z*ebra + *sc*issors
24.	zh	ž	ʒ	televi*s*ion

encourage the development of symbol-sound or grapheme-phoneme correspondences to achieve decoding skill.

Reexamining Table 1, one notes that the i.t.a. system uses four additional, and seemingly redundant, letters, one each for the /k/, /r/, /w/, and /z/ phonemes. From the standpoint of identifying the phoneme, such redundancy holds. However, these letters are used to provide for ease in transition to traditionally printed words and, as such, are not redundant. Moreover, one of them, /ꞷh/, helps to suggest that some linguists would also broaden the consonant table to include at least one more symbol, /ʍ/. This upside down *w* is often used by linguists to represent the diphthong in the initial position of such words as *why, whether,* or *while.* This diphthong is typically represented by the reversed *wh* /hw/ to encode the aspirated *h* before *w* heard in the speech of many Americans.

All three systems agree on the number of consonant phonemes that need to be represented for the instruction of children. Although they vary in symbolization, they are in accord that there are twenty-four significant consonant phonemes and that none will be considered diphthongal for instructional purposes. These agreements are paralleled by most dictionary writers.

It is difficult, though possible, to define a consonant phoneme as distinct from a vowel phoneme since the distinction between consonants and vowels is largely arbitrary and becomes obscured in the so-called semivowels. The term *consonant* means "sounded with," whereas *vowel* means "voice."

Vowel sounds are made by leaving a space between the tongue and the palate and then allowing air to pass through the space while, simultaneously, the vocal chords are vibrating. The quality of vowel sounds is also partly determined by the position of the lips. Consonants, on the other hand, are made by exploding air past the lips, sounding through the nose, filtering air through tooth-gaps, working air between the lips, or rubbing air past the tongue tip and roof of the mouth. The consonant /h/, as in *hat*, however, is a pure breath sound, whereas /y/ as in *yes* and /w/ as in *well* have some of the characteristics of vowels and consonants; that is, they are neither completely a consonant nor a vowel and are called semivowels. In general, consonants and vowels can be distinguished in terms of the way they are physically produced. When one stands before a mirror and examines one's lips and mouth while pronouncing any series of words, one can see that the consonants represent an obstruction or momentary stoppage in the continuous flow of air, whereas vowels are made with relatively open and unimpeded positions of the mouth organs.

Consonants can be said to be the backbone of speech and, in written language, lead the reader to recognize the words that are intended. For example, the sentence "The rain in Spain stays mainly in the plain" is recognized when the vowels are omitted, Th__ r____n __n Sp____n st____s m____nl__ __n th__ pl____n, but it is unintelligible when the consonants are omitted, ____e __ai__ i__ ____ai__ ____ay__ __ai____y __n ____e ____ai__. Perhaps this is the reason why children in spelling rarely omit consonants but often omit vowels.

In summary, a consonant is a speech-sound made with more or less obstruction of the breath stream; a vowel is a speech-sound produced without obstructing the flow of air.

THE VOWEL PHONEMES

The vowel phonemes, as listed in Table 2, demonstrate that the three systems presented in Table 1 are here in basic agreement on the number of vowel phonemes that need to be symbolized. Un-

TABLE 2. Vowel Phonemes as Symbolized by Three Systems

	Phonemic	Soffietti	Other	i.t.a.(Adapted)	Key Word
1.	a	æ		a	apple
2.	ā	e	(ey)	æ	angel
3.	a	a		o (+a)#	octopus
4.	e	ɛ		e	Eskimo
5.	ē	i	(iy)	ɛɛ	eagle
6.	i	ɪ		i	Indian
7.	Ō	o	(uw)	œ	boat
8.	ȯ	ɔ		aʋ	automobile
9.	ü	u		ω	shoe
10.	u̇	ʋ		ω	book
11.	ə	ə		u	sure
12.				(a)#	father

	Phonemic	Soffietti	Other	i.t.a.	
	Diphthongs	Phonemic	Clusters	Vowels	Key Word
1.	au̇	aʋ	(aw)	ou	owl
2.	I	aɪ	(ay)	ie	ice
3.	oi	ɔɪ	(auy)	oi	boy
4.	yü	ɪu	(yω)	ue	unite
5.		ə	(ur)		girl

fortunately, linguists, professors, and reading experts disagree not only on the terminology and classification of vowel phonemes but also on the number of vowel phonemes in the language. As already shown, at least thirty-six vowel phonemes could exist. However, this number has no relevance to instruction in reading. Instead, we should recognize that only a minimal number of phonemes are semantically functional to the nonspecialist and that only these few need to be symbolized. The remainder helps the language specialist in distinguishing regional or local dialects.

Although Table 2 indicates basic agreements, it also shows why disagreements among anagnologists (reading specialists, experts, etc.) exist as well as the specific points of disagreement. The i.t.a. system, for example, identifies sixteen vowel phonemes. Each system agrees on eleven basic vowel phonemes, but the i.t.a. column includes a twelfth not found in the others. The phoneme /ɑ/, father, is often considered to be no or little different from the third phoneme /o/, octopus, and is often considered to be merely an allophone of /o/. Thus, it is not found in either of the other two systems.

Although I do not personally distinguish between these two vowels in my idiolect, the use of /ɑ/, father, is understandable since i.t.a., unlike the other alphabets, is used for transitional purposes and as a single alphabet to represent the phonemes of all English-speaking peoples. British speakers most often distinguish between these two phonemes. If *fothur* were written for *father*, even a British child would have no difficulty in understanding which word was meant. The difference between the two sounds /o/, octopus, /ɑ/, father, is so small that the use of one rather than two phonemes presents no impediment to instruction. While there is value in using the second symbol in an initial learning medium, it has little value here and may be ignored. Alternatively, we can use the symbols interchangeably and may distinguish between them for reading instruction (see Chapter 3).

There are eleven vowel phonemes universally recognized as important for reading instruction, though one might be confused by symbols used to represent them. The phonemic system is most like the one used in some dictionaries; the second, Soffietti's, uses symbols of the international phonetic alphabet; and i.t.a. uses symbols that closely parallel ligatured letters of traditional English print. (For the moment, the column headed "Other" will not be considered.) Whereas i.t.a. uses the symbol æ, a combination of *a* and *e*, to represent the phoneme /æ/ as found in the initial position of *a*ngel, Soffietti uses the same symbol to represent the vowel phoneme heard in the words *hat*, *fat*, and *cat*. The i.t.a. symbols will be used here to represent the phonemes of English since they most closely parallel familiar and high-frequency spellings of traditional print media and have been found to be most easily learned and used for such spellings by teachers and reading specialists.

As Table 2 shows, there are at least four additional phonemes (for a total of fifteen) on which there is basic agreement—the phonemes heard in the initial position of the words *owl*, *ice*, *boy*, and *unite*—and these are variously identified as diphthongs, phonemic clusters, or vowels. When you recall that diphthong was identified earlier as meaning two sounds, you will also understand by reference to the column headed "Other" how these sounds could be written in i.t.a. and that the i.t.a. system has simplified the child's learning by not using such terms as long, short, broad, or diphthongal to distinguish between the vowels. The other systems would, on the other hand, minimally identify certain phonemes as vowels and diphthongs or vowels and phonemic clusters while ignoring the diphthongal or phonemic character nature of vowels 2, 5, and 7. Herein lies one of the major discrepancies in the field of reading.

If there are in fact diphthongs in the vowel system, then there also must be monophthongs and triphthongs as well. The vowels typically identified as long vowels in most instructional texts for teachers or children are considered to have both monophthongal (one-sound) and diphthongal (two-sound) variations (see Kenyon and Knott, 1953), but linguists and phoneticians generally identify the speech-sounds heard in the initial position of the words *angel, eagle, oat, ice, unite, owl,* and *oyster* as diphthongal.

The use of *y* and *w* in combination with a simple vowel can be further clarified at this point. The speech-sounds represented by *y* and *w* are called semivowels because they are closely related to vowels; they are, however, often called *glides*. A glide is understood to be a rapid movement of the articulatory organs of speech to or from the position they take for the articulation of a certain vowel. The glide [y] in *yo-yo* is related to the vowel [e] in *bell* in this way, and the glide [w], *w*agon, to (ω), b*oot*. The pronunciation of the word *wow*, for example, starts from the articulatory position used to pronounce [ω], b*oot*, with the lips rounded and the tongue in a high back position. Instead of articulating [ω], however, the vocal organs glide rapidly into position for [o], as in p*o*t; as the [o] is being pronounced, the lips and tongue glide back where they came from so that the word *wow* ends as the lips and tongue approach the [ω] position.

Glides are often, though not always, related to what are called the high vowels, with [w] and [y] being the most common. The vowels /æ/, *a*ngel, and /œ/, g*oa*t, are usually pronounced with the accompanying glide, and thus it is correct to show these sounds as a vowel plus *y* or *w*: /ey/ and /ow/. The words *paid* and *goat* would be written phonetically as /peyd/ and /gowt/. Each of the three systems used here, however, ignores these glides and represents the initial sound in *a*ngel as [a, e, æ], the initial sound in *ea*gle as [e, i, ɛɛ], and the initial sound in *oa*ts as [o, o, œ].

The column titled "Other" attempts to identify for the reader how the glides might be represented. You'll remember that y and w were identified as semivowels and that by adding the y and w to the simple vowels, other complex sounds could be symbolized. Out of the eighteen possible combinations of a simple vowel and either y or w, seven complex vowel phonemes have been identified as semantically functional and included by all three systems: /æ/ = /ey/, /ɛɛ/ = /iy/, /œ/ = /uw/, /au/ = /aw/, /ie/ = /ay/, /ɔi/ = /auy/, and /ue/ = /yꙮ/, among the total of fifteen. However, the last of the list is not a vowel *plus* y or w; instead, the y precedes the vowel sound and is often identified as an inglided vowel phoneme.

By this point, the reader should see that the term *long vowel* has always identified certain vowel sounds that are more clearly understood as being diphthongs but not always identified as such, and that long vowels, according to definitions used thus far, are synonymous with diphthongs, or phonemic clusters, and also with glided vowels.

Kenyon and Knott (1953), in their *Pronouncing Dictionary of American English,* provide a rationale for identifying /æ/, /ɛɛ/, and /œ/ as simple vowels and thereby justify the inclusion of these sounds among the eleven basic vowel sounds listed in Table 2. Kenyon and Knott point out that /æ/, /ɛɛ/, and /œ/ are monophthongal in *vacation, radio,* and *obey* and diphthongal in *way, bee,* and *toe.* It would appear that these vowel sounds have monophthongal usage more often than not but that /ie/, *i*ce, /ue/, *u*nite, /ɔu/, *o*wl, and /ɔi/, *o*yster are always diphthongal in usage, justifying their identification separately.

Although early classification procedures have labeled certain vowels as long, short, broad, and diphthongal, they have not been accurate since certain "long" vowels, /ie/ and /ue/, should have been included among the diphthongs; or, if "long" was intended to supplant the need to use the word *diphthong,* then /ɔu/ and /ɔi/ should have been identified as "long" vowels. The word *long* in relation to a classification of vowels can only be understood in this way since the length of a "long" vowel—that is, the amount of time needed to produce the sound /æ/, *a*ngel, as opposed to /a/, *c*at—is no greater. A difference in length or duration of vowel sounds does exist, for example, in the words *sat* and *sand.* For phonetic purposes, this difference in the second case is written /sa:nd/. However, that time difference does not exist between the phonemes /a/ or /æ/ in the words *sat* and *sate.*

Similarly, later classification systems that use the terms *glided* and *unglided vowels* produce confusion when they add a further modification by labeling some vowel phonemes as vowel consonant glides. Since the vowels have been identified as representing a simple vowel plus a glide, or semivowel, and a glide, or semivowel, is known to be either *w* or *y*, the vowel phonemes /æ/, /ɛɛ/, /œ/, and /ie/ are as much vowel consonant glides as are /ɔu/ or /ɔi/, which are identified in the *Ginn 360* materials as the only vowel consonant glides. This set of materials adds a further confusion when it includes /ue/ in the same category as /ɔu/ and /ie/ and labels it a vowel consonant glide. It is obvious that this complex vowel phoneme begins with the consonant (semivowel, or glide) /y/ and ends with the articulatory position of /ɷ/.

If reading instructors require anything more than a twofold classification (consonants and vowels) of the phonemes of English, better and more accurate definitions of terms are needed. However, since distinguishing between vowel phonemes in the acquisition stage of reading skill has little instructional value, such distinctions seem pointless. Indeed, they would only confuse children who may use different materials and different classification systems in the course of their early school careers. A child could know how to decode all the vowel phonemes from early instruction in one school and yet be graded wrong in his or her workbooks in a new school that uses a set of special terms.

Table 2 shows that Soffietti includes one additional complex vowel phoneme /ur/, which he labels a phonemic cluster. Most reading instructional systems call attention to the vowel plus *r* in such words as *her, fur, sir,* and *myrtle* but do not further classify these phoneme sequences or, if they do, refer to the "influence *r*" or to "vowels influenced by *r*."

The phoneme /r/ is identified by phoneticians as one of two *liquid* consonants, /r/ and /l/, in English. The /l/ phoneme is identified as a lateral sound since in the word *lip* the tongue's position is against the front of the roof of the mouth and air escapes on the sides. Since the flow of air is continuous, it resembles a vowel in quality.

The /r/, as in *ring*, involves no closure of the speech organs and therefore is very much like a vowel. Either the front or rear of the tongue is raised slightly toward the roof of the mouth so that the upper surface is shaped like a cup. Rather than affecting the quality of the preceding vowel sound in the word *her*, it would appear that the /r/ is dragged across the mouth by the preceding vowel sound. The sound before /r/ in the words *her* and *sir* and in both vowel positions in *mother* is the same as the vowel sound in *sun*. As seen in columns 1 and 2 of Table 2, it is written as an inverted backward *e*, to represent what is called the *schwa* sound.

Technically, the *schwa* sound refers only to the unglided /u/, s*u*n, when heard in unaccented syllables. Although some phoneticians insist that the /u/ in both vowel positions in *mother*, /mu*t*hur/, are distinctly different, this difference is ignored by others as being merely allophonic. Since, in working with children, differences are simplified for purposes of decoding, such differences here and in decoding instruction are ignored.

Soffietti's inclusion of /ər/ as a phonemic cluster is merely the /u/ of *sun* followed by /r/. Since the phonemes exist separately, no significant benefit is experienced by including /ər/ as a semantically functional unit in Table 2.

Soffietti would indicate sixteen vowel phonemes, including /ur/; i.t.a. does not recognize /ur/ with a special symbol but discriminates between /o/, p*o*t, and /ɑ/, f*a*ther; and the phonemic alphabet rejects both of these. The commonality of fifteen vowel phonemes in all three systems is undoubtedly the minimal number of vowel phonemes that need attention in general instruction. When added to the twenty-four consonant phonemes, a total of thirty-nine phonemes are identified in the English language as important for use with beginning readers. The distinction between the *a* in *father* and the *o* in *pot* can be ignored or treated as an important dialect difference. By adding the vowel sounds in *air* and making fine distinctions such as that /u/ is different in s*o*n, h*u*rt, and lab*o*r, lexicographers indicate a forty-four-sound base. Some others will add the /ɛɛ/ in *here* as different from the /ɛɛ/ in *he* and eliminate one distinction of /u/. Such distinctions are not considered here.

At this point, let us clarify symbol-to-sound and grapheme-phoneme correspondences. Some anagnologists hold that we all have a concept of each of the letters of the alphabet. These concepts have developed from multiple variations of the symbol in print. For this reason, some authors use the term *symbol* to refer to a specific example of a letter, whereas still others use the word *character*. Linguists generally use the term *grapheme* to describe the concept level, although not all are comfortable with this usage. Most people would agree that a letter is one of the signs conventionally used in writing and printing to represent speech-sounds, or that it refers to an alphabetic character. Since, in teaching reading, we often use the word *digraph* to mean two letters or two letters that represent one sound different from that represented by either letter, the terms *graphs* and *trigraphs* should probably be used as well. It would appear that a system comparable to that used to describe the speech-sounds of English (phone, allophone, phoneme) is available for referring more precisely to the printed or cursive forms of a letter as well as for referring to combinations of letters used to represent a speech-sound. Thus, in the word *read,* there are three graphemes *r-ea-d* representing the phonemes /r/-/ɛɛ/-/d/.

HOW PHONETIC IS AMERICAN ENGLISH?

The question refers to the general practice of determining how much agreement there is between the spelling and the sounds of a language, and the answer should, ordinarily, be simply derived. Having agreed that there are a maximum of 39 (or at best 44 as distinguished in adult dictionaries) consonant and vowel phonemes in the language, it would appear that all we would have to do is determine the number of spellings we use to represent the phonemes and, by dividing the number of spellings into the number of phonemes, come up with a result. This is the procedure commonly used to compare the phonetic quality of languages from one country to another. American writers frequently reject this procedure since the English language proves to be less than 1 percent phonetic under this procedure, and such an admission would ordinarily preclude recommending a phonic emphasis in reading instruction.

Comparing languages on their grapheme-phoneme correspondences, Spanish, Finnish, and Italian are found to be almost wholly phonetic, whereas German is 90 percent phonetic and Russian 94 percent phonetic. Italian, for example, has twenty-seven phonemes and twenty-eight letters or combinations of letters used to represent them (three pairs of two phonemes use the same letter to represent their sounds, and the few cases with more than one spelling are governed by specific rules). By dividing twenty-seven by twenty-eight, Italian is seen to be 96 percent phonetic.

But what of English? The tables of common English spellings found in many unabridged dictionaries show that as many as 340 to 360 spellings are listed for the 44 phonemes these dictionaries typically use; the result suggests that English is 12 to 13 percent phonetic. A collegiate dictionary such as the *American College Dictionary* shows 289 different spellings for the 44 phonemes of English, a

15 percent phonetic result. Perhaps we need go no further since the statement used by many authors, that 85 percent of words (or portions of words) in English are regularly spelled and therefore phonetic, while 15 percent are not; but the 15 percent which are not are used 85 percent of the time, provides us with all the information we need. Particularly so since the statement tells us what the above division of grapheme-phoneme correspondences produced. Yet the key word, *common,* used by the *American College Dictionary* in *A Table of Common English Spellings*, tells us that these spellings are not the only spellings.

Dewey's 1923 study of the spellings of English sounds identified 547 different spellings (1923, 1970), whereas Heuser's (1974) replication of this study showed only 421. Dewey's result, using 44 sounds, indicated English is less than 1 percent phonetic, and Heuser's result allows us to say English is a little better than 1 percent phonetic. Moving to the lower number of phonemes (39), we can show that English is, according to the various counts, 0.7 percent (Dewey), 0.9 percent (Heuser), or 13 percent *(American College Dictionary)* phonetic. With fewer spellings admitted and more phonemes, we find English is, at best, 15 percent phonetic and, at worst, less than 1 percent phonetic. Only the last figure would ordinarily be acceptable based on usual comparative procedures.

Moore (1951) attempted a determination of the validity of the Bloomfield (1933) statement that large numbers of words contain highly consistent phoneme-grapheme relationships. Using the 3,000 most frequently used American English words, his research demonstrated that 80 percent of 12,546 phonemes represented in those words were spelled consistently. Horn (1962), however, challenged Moore's conclusion, maintaining that the less frequently used words, those beyond the 3,000-word sample analyzed by Moore, might show less consistency. Using a 10,000-word sample and a research design intended to eliminate methodological weaknesses in Moore's research, Horn produced results that refuted Moore's findings.

Hanna et al. (1966), aided by computer technology and using a body of 17,310 different words "representative of the total American-English lexicon of an educated U.S. citizen" (1966:13), did even more extensive research. They devised a 52-phoneme code and identified 377 different spellings for these phonemes. Although simple division produces a result of close to 14 percent, similar to the "at best" results reported earlier, the authors did not content themselves with this finding. These authors reported that only 6

(27 percent) of the 22 vowel phonemes equaled or exceeded their 80 percent criterion for demonstrating the alphabetic principle of phoneme-grapheme correspondence, whereas 19 (63 percent) of the 30 consonant phonemes met this criterion. It was also demonstrated that when 203 rules — including the position of the phoneme (initial, medial, or final), whether the syllable was accented or not, and the environment of the phoneme (that is, what phonemes preceded or followed it) — were developed and fed into the computer, the computer could spell correctly the 17,009 (of 17,310) words it attempted with only 50 percent accuracy. If one to three spelling errors were tolerated, then the computer could spell with 100 percent accuracy. Although we can agree with these authors' conclusion that English is essentially alphabetically based, the point seems obvious to begin with.

The authors of this study, however, further conclude that "for 90 percent of the phonemes in the language, the orthography approaches the 1 to 1 ideal to the ratio of 77:52 when all phonological factors are considered" (Hanna et al., 1966:121), that is, the 203 rules. On this basis (knowing the 203 rules), we can conclude that English is almost 68 percent phonetic. However, such a conclusion is invalid since only 90 percent of phonemes are used, since no phonological factors are considered for other language comparisons, since linguists question the clarity or distinctions between the phonemes identified for the study, and since there is no evidence that adults, let alone children, are capable of learning (or have to any great extent done so in the absence of instruction) the full range of generalizations used in this study. In fact, "no member of the research team would advocate that these rules be memorized and used in a deductive manner by elementary school children" (Hanna et al., 1966:123).

American English spelling is essentially nonphonetic, or minimally so at best, with estimates of the phonetic nature of spelling ranging from a low of 1 percent to a high of 15 percent. Although this is generally agreed upon, some linguists argue that while English may not be phonetic at the phoneme-grapheme level, it is more phonetic than some people realize when the morpho-phonemic level is considered.

A phoneme is the smallest semantically functional unit of speech, whereas a *morpheme* is the smallest linguistic unit with a meaning of its own. The morpheme can be a phoneme or composed of more than one phoneme. The word-partials usually labeled as *roots*, *prefixes,* or *suffixes* are morphemes, as are such words as *a* and *I* when either considered as single phonemes or identified as diphthongs.

The word *cats* consists of two morphemes, /c a t/ and /s/, since /s/ carries the plural meaning, whereas the word *unfinished* consists of three morphemes, /un/ /finiʃh/ /t/. The morphemes /cat/ and /finiʃh/ have lexical meaning, whereas /s/, /un/, and /t/ have relational meaning. *Lexical meaning* refers to abstract or concrete persons, things, happenings, and so on, and *relational meaning* refers to time, place, and so on. The morpheme /z/ of /hɛɛrz/ (hears), for example, has the relational meaning of "present tense, singular number" and is considered a bound morpheme. A *bound morpheme* merely refers to the fact that it cannot stand alone and retain meaning. *Free morphemes,* such as /cat/ and /finish/, can stand alone and have a meaning of their own.

Morpho-phonemic refers to those characteristics of words such as *hymn, bomb,* or perhaps even *partial* in which the *n, b* and often *i* are considered silent letters and would not appear in a phonemic notation; /him/, /bom/, /parʃhul/. However, the functions, according to Weir and Venezky (1968:189), of *n, b,* and *i* are to preserve a morphemic pattern as revealed in the words *hymnal, bombast,* or *partiality,* where the *n, b,* and *i* are pronounced. In the Weir and Venezky (1968) study "English Orthography—More Reasons Than Rhyme," a computer tabulation of the grapheme-phoneme correspondences found in the most common 20,000 English words was undertaken to determine the types of relationships that were reflected in the orthography. One of the most important distinctions they identified was that between relation units (those letters that are morpho-phonemic) and markers (letters that serve to indicate the correspondences of other letters). They reiterate what Francis (1958) had suggested earlier, that the "silent *e*" functions as a marker in such words as *give, cake,* or *since.* This notion suggests that the *e* in *give* preserves a *graphotactic* (a rule in writing) pattern since *v* is not allowed in the final position of words; that the *e* in *cake* marks the pronunciation of *a* as being the *a* in *angel;* and that in *since* the *e* marks the correspondence of *c* to /s/.

While Weir and Venezky (1968:198) indicate that "simple grapheme-to-phoneme correspondences are unproductive for the prediction of sound from spelling" and call for the use of phonemic, morphemic and morpho-phonemic patterns as the best descriptive approach of the spelling-to-sound correspondences of the language, no relevant data are provided to answer the question of how phonetic English is. Useful information on correspondences can help children develop decoding skill in relation to intricate English spellings, but the history of English spellings has been marked by etymological error and bias, and thus these spellings are today needlessly complex and inconsistent. In short, learning to decode print into sound in the acquisition stage of reading requires learning not only grapheme-phoneme correspondences but also morphemes, sight vocabulary, and relational, marker, and other generalizations as well.

HISTORY OF PHONICS IN READING INSTRUCTION

Although Huey (1968:265) wrote at the beginning of this century, his statement that "the methods of learning to read that are in common use today may be classed as alphabetic, phonic, phonetic, word, sentence, and combination methods" still holds. In the some 130 sets of books, workbooks, and other instructional materials currently available, all the methods he identified are used or recommended for use in some combination.

The alphabet method used in early Greece and Rome found almost universal favor in Europe and the United States well into the nineteenth century. Discarded for a time, it appears active on the current scene in the modern-dress version of materials for instruction such as *Alpha One: Breaking the Code* (1970). Early descriptions of the method emphasized teaching the names of the printed letters as well as the sequence of the letters in the alphabet. Huey (1968:265 – 266) points out: "Sometimes the sounds of the letters are also taught. Then nonsense syllables like *ab, ib, ob* are spelled and pronounced; then combinations of three letters, monosyllabic words, disyllables, etc., follows, the word usually being spelled before it is pronounced."

In recent years, recommendations to teach the letter names have been based on research interpreted as demonstrating that the single most important ability in reading achievement is the child's knowledge of the names of the letters of the alphabet. However, when it was discovered that the names of the letters were not significant although the sounds which the letters represented and inherent in letter names were, such recommendations were questioned (Samuels, 1969).

Certainly, the child who is constantly involved with letters often acquires a familiarity with the sounds represented by them. As such, the alphabet method always utilized something of phonics as well.

The alphabet method was modified as early as 1534 in Europe toward what has been called phonetics but is really what we call phonics. Hall (1874:2) reports that Ickelsamer used a procedure of "placing the picture of an animal, its printed name, and the letter whose sound was most like the animal's voice or cry in parallel columns. Against the picture of a dog, for example, was placed the growling r, against a bird the twittering z," and so on. The method was later amplified to include the association of a with apple, b with boy, and the like. Anyone familiar with today's materials will surely recognize these procedures as being similar to those used in the alphabet books of many publishers.

In a curious method used in Germany, schoolboys assumed the character of letters in dress or actions (twisting their bodies into the shape of various letters). Some modern imitations of this exist. In both early and modern versions, there is a loss of attention to the letter's name; instead, the focus is on its sound or visual form.

The straightforward phonic method apparently advocated initially by the Jansenists was advocated again in 1790 by Thornton but neglected until revived by Isaac Pitman in 1855 and later in the "Pronouncing Orthography" of Edwin Leigh in 1864. In the earliest phonic methods, words were spelled by producing the succession of sounds forming them. American authors, recognizing that there were not enough letters in the twenty-six-letter alphabet to represent the sounds of English, added new characters so that each sound could be represented. These alphabets were identified as phonetic methods and enjoyed great success initially.

Leigh's "Pronouncing Orthography" used special forms to represent the different sounds. Sometimes these forms were only a slight modification of the regular letter. Silent letters were printed in skeleton print or in hair lines. The system, patented by Leigh, was used in a series of readers, including that of McGuffey. However, the system fell into disfavor since it apparently was hard on the eyes and required a close inspection of the letters in order to distinguish between them. This spelling method was not unlike that recommended by Jansenists. Words were spelled by the succession of sounds and not by letter names. The word was slowly pronounced until the child became aware of its sounds, and these sounds were then associated with the symbols used to represent them. One feature of this procedure, that of training the child to articulate given sounds, apparently was appealing; as Smith (1965:69) points out, emphasis was placed "upon articulation and pronunciation as a means of correcting the numerous dialects that had sprung up in different sections, and of bringing about a greater unity of the American language."

The word method, first suggested as an approach for reading instruction by Comenius in 1658 in *Orbis Pictus*, the first illustrated schoolbook, also found favor with Horace Mann, among others, in the United States. During the first half of the twentieth century, it appeared to become the dominant method; and during this same period, phonics was neglected. While context clues and structural analysis were added as techniques for working out pronunciation of words, only a limited amount of phonics was recommended in the first grade. Witty (1942:106) pointed out the apparent reasons for this, noting that

> experimentation on the teaching of phonics has led to contradictory claims and some confusion over the value of phonic principles in "unlocking" new words. Nor is there agreement concerning the nature or numbers of the specific units to be taught, nor the levels at which the various units should be introduced. In general, the practice followed in modern schools is to delay phonics analysis of words until children have a start in reading for meaning and a stock of sight words.

For a long time, teachers did not accept the idea that phonics was a valuable approach to word recognition. But in 1955, Flesch, in *Why Johnny Can't Read*, suggested that teachers had been poorly taught and that the basal readers had wholly abandoned this valuable approach. Ironically, while Flesch indicated abandonment, every manual that accompanied basal readers of this period recognized the need for phonic instruction and outlined procedures for teaching it. In the 1960s, the argument by proponents and opponents of phonics shifted in emphasis to a discussion of how early such information should be given. Both the Columbia-Carnegie (Barton and Wilder, 1962) and Harvard (Austin and Coleman, 1963) studies found that some sort of phonics as well as the whole-word method were universally taught. Barton and Wilder (1962:173) in the Columbia-Carnegie study reported:

In the first grade, 90% of the classes "learn new words as wholes" on half or more of the days; and 82% of the classes "learn to sound out words from letters and letter combinations" on half or more of the days. A variety of word recognition practices are used.

Nonetheless, the argument continued, with meaning-emphasis (another term for a look-say beginning for word learning) advocates losing ground to phonic or strong-code-emphasis proponents. The latter were viewed with increasing favor owing to social pressures on the schools to improve instruction in general as a result of the Russian launching of the Sputnik satellite. It was pointed out that

> In looking at the reading process, we seem to have been looking too long at comprehension as the basis for a definition of reading English; however, comprehension is primarily the *goal* of the reading activity. Meaning is less important as a clue to word recognition in other language systems; in English, comprehension turns out to be one of the major clues to word recognition. In effect, the definition of reading under which we've operated has focused on the purpose of reading rather than its nature. We quite naturally stressed meaning, which is the goal of reading, at the expense of the process. (Mazurkiewicz, 1964)

The issue of early or late phonic institution has not yet been resolved, and there still exist numerous adherents of a later emphasis. Often, these adherents raise objections such as that an early phonic emphasis *might* cause a slow reading rate in later years, though no research ever demonstrated any justification for such a belief. In fact, longitudinal research (Mazurkiewicz, 1975) supports an early decoding emphasis.

Chall's (1967) advocacy of a code emphasis rather than a meaning emphasis as had been advocated by authors of basal readers for forty or more years was based on a review of selected studies that compared the effects on pupil achievement of differing amounts of phonics. Although most readers assume that the study attempted to lay to rest the argument of a look-say beginning versus a phonic beginning, others view this Carnegie Foundation—supported study as a comparison of early or late phonic instruction. In fact, the research that Chall examined in her study included look-say beginnings with varying amounts of phonics (from little or no phonics to intrinsic phonics) as well as early and strong phonic emphasis that she equated with code learning. Her conclusions indicate:

> The research from 1912 to 1965 indicates that a code-emphasis method— i.e., one that views beginning reading as essentially different from mature

reading and emphasizes learning of the printed code for the spoken language—produces better results, at least up to the point where sufficient evidence seems to be available, the end of the third grade.

The results are better, not only in terms of the mechanical aspects of literacy alone, as was once supposed, but also in terms of the ultimate goal of reading instruction, comprehension, and possibly even speed of reading. The long-existing fear that an initial code emphasis produces readers who do not read for meaning or with enjoyment is unfounded. On the contrary, the evidence indicates that better results in terms of reading for meaning are achieved with the programs that emphasize code at the start than with the programs that stress meaning at the beginning. (Chall, 1967:307)

Chall's conclusions do not suggest that sight vocabulary, look-say, or meaning-getting are to be ignored, nor do they suggest that a code emphasis must precede and may not be accompanied by other instructional procedures. To suggest otherwise, as some authors do, would be to denigrate the effectiveness of the Chall study. Chall does suggest that her analysis "tends to support Bloomfield's definition that the first step in learning to read one's national language is essentially learning a printed code for the speech we possess" (1967:83). As will be seen later, this writer subscribes to both conclusions and will recommend a program of decoding that includes such an emphasis from the outset of instruction.

REFERENCES

Alpha One: Breaking the Code. Jericho, N.Y.: New Dimensions in Education, Inc., 1970.

Austin, Mary C., and Coleman, Morrison. *The First R.* New York: Macmillan, 1963.

Barton, Allen, and Wilder, David. "Columbia-Carnegie Study of Reading Research and Its Communication." *Proceedings of the International Reading Association.* New York: Scholastic Magazine Press, 1962.

Betts, Emmet A. "Orthography: Phonemes and Dictionary Respelling." *Spelling Progress Bulletin* 14 (Fall 1974): 13–14.

Bloomfield, Leonard. *Language.* New York: Holt, 1933.

Chall, Jeanne. *Learning to Read: The Great Debate.* New York: McGraw-Hill, 1967.

Dewey, Godfrey. *Relative Frequency of English Spellings.* New York: Columbia University, Teachers College Press, 1970.

Flesch, Rudolf. *Why Johnny Can't Read.* New York: Harper & Bros., 1955.

Francis, W. Nelson. *The Structure of American English.* New York: Ronald Press, 1958.

Hall, G. S. *How to Teach Reading and What to Read in Schools.* Boston: Heath, 1874.

Hanna, Paul R., et al. *Phoneme-Grapheme Correspondences as Cues to Spelling Improvement.* Washington, D.C.: U.S. Office of Education, Bureau of Research, 1966.

Heuser, Elizabeth. *Phoneme-Grapheme Correspondences Reexamined.* Master's thesis, Kean College, Union, N.J., 1974.

Horn, Thomas D. "The Effect of the Corrected Test on Learning to Spell." *The Elementary School Journal* 47 (1962): 277–285.

Huey, Edmund Burke. *The Psychology and Pedagogy of Reading.* Boston: Macmillan, 1908. Reprinted. Cambridge, Mass.: MIT Press, 1968.

Kenyon, John S., and Knott, Thomas A. *A Pronouncing Dictionary of American English.* Springfield, Mass.: Merriam, 1953.

Mazurkiewicz, A. J. "A Tiger by the Tail." *Proceedings of 29th Educational Conference.* New York: Educational Records Bureau, 1964.

————. "Comparative Attitudes and Achievements of the 1963 i.t.a. and T.O. Taught Students in the Tenth and Eleventh Grades." *Reading World* 14 (1975): 242–251.

Moore, James T., Jr. "Phonetic Elements Appearing in a Three Thousand Word Spelling Vocabulary." Ph.D. dissertation, Stanford University, School of Education, 1951.

Pitman, Sir James, with Mazurkiewicz, A. J., and Tanyzer, H. J. *The Handbook on Writing and Spelling in i.t.a.* New York: i/t/a Publications, 1964.

Samuels, S. J. "Word Recognition and Beginning Reading." *The Reading Teacher* 23 (November 1969): 159–161.

Smith, Nila B. *American Reading Instruction.* Newark, Del.: International Reading Association, 1965.

Soffietti, James. "Why Children Fail to Read: A Linguistic Analysis." In *New Perspectives in Reading Instruction,* edited by A. J. Mazurkiewicz. New York: Pitman, 1968.

Weir, R., and Venezky, R. "English Orthography—More Reasons Than Rhyme." In *The Psycholinguistic Nature of the Reading Process,* edited by Kenneth Goodman. Detroit: Wayne State University Press, 1968.

Witty, Paul. *Reading for Interest.* Boston: Heath, 1942.

3

The Consonants

A consonant is both a speech-sound produced with more or less obstruction of the breath stream and a letter used to represent such a speech-sound. Twenty-four consonant phonemes must be symbolized in order to express those sounds in print for a child's identification. Most people would agree that there are twenty-one consonant letters in the alphabet: *b, c, d, f, g, h, j, k, l, m, n, p, q, r, s, t, v, w, x, y,* and *z.* However, this enumeration neglects usage since some consonant letters do not represent only consonant sounds. The semivowels *h, w,* and *y* are used as both consonants and vowels. Thus, it would seem more accurate to say that there are eighteen consonant letters in the alphabet, plus, at times, *h, w,* and *y.* Unfortunately, this is not the whole story either, since *e, i, u,* and *o* represent the consonant sounds /y/, azal*e*a and un*i*on, and /w/, s*u*ave and ch*o*ir. Once again the statement must be modified: there are eighteen consonant letters, with *h, i, u, w,* and *y* being used often. The very infrequent usages of *o* to represent /w/ in ch*o*ir, mem*o*ir, repert*o*ire, and *o*ne and the single usage of *e* to represent the /y/ in azal*e*a are omitted since they are irrelevant to a primary vocabulary, though they are obviously not ignored. The *o* in *one* is

considered by most lexicographers to represent the /wu/ phonemes.

Only one letter appears to represent vowel sounds alone: *a*.
(See Chapter 4 for a further discussion.) The letter *y*, for example,
is used as vowel some 97 percent of the time. We've obviously
been misled by instruction to accept the notion that *y*'s usage is
principally that of a consonant and, in turn, misleading to children
in discussing this particular letter let alone neglectful of the frequent
consonantal usages of *i* and *u*.

Table 3 identifies the twenty-four significant consonant phonemes and the graphemes used to represent those phonemes in
print. Two phonemes, /th/ and /th/, are each represented by only
one grapheme in the orthography, whereas others are represented
by many more—fourteen different graphemes for /k/, and nineteen
for /ʃh/. The table also reveals that many graphemes are used to
represent several different phonemes: *g* represents /g/, /j/ and /ʒ/;
t represents /ch/, /ʃh/, and /ʒ/; *s* represents /s/, /ʃh/, /z/ and /ʒ/.

A comparison with the nearly phonetic Italian alphabet reveals
that whereas American English uses at least 176 graphemes to
represent the 24 consonant phonemes (roughly 14 percent phonetic), with an average 7.3 graphemes for each phoneme, Italian

TABLE 3. Consonant Phonemes and Their Most Frequent Spellings

	Phoneme	*Graphemes*	*Examples*
1.	/b/	b, bb, pb	*by*, ru*bb*er, cu*pb*oard
2.	/ch/	c, ch, t, tch, te th, ti	*c*ello, whi*ch*, situa*t*ion, ma*tch*, righ*te*ous, pos*th*umous, ques*ti*on
3.	/d/	d, dd, ed, ld	an*d*, a*dd*, call*ed*, wou*ld*
4.	/f/	f, ff, ft, gh, lf, ph, pph	*f*or, o*ff*, o*f*ten, enou*gh*, ha*lf*, gra*ph*ic, sa*pph*ire
5.	/g/	g, gg, gh, ½x*	*g*ood, e*gg*, *gh*ost, e*x*act
6.	/h/	h, wh, ½wh	*h*is, *wh*o, *wh*ich
7.	/j/	d, de, dg, di, dj	e*d*ucation, gran*de*ur, knowl- e*dg*e, sol*di*er, a*dj*ust
8.	/k/	c, cc, cch, ch, ck, cq, k, kh, lk, q, sc, x, ½x, ½xi	*c*an a*cc*ord, ba*cch*anal, *sch*ool, ba*ck*, la*cq*uer, *k*ind, *kh*aki, ta*lk*, *q*uite, vis*c*ount, e*x*cept, ne*x*t, no*xi*ous
9.	/l/	cl, l, ½le, ll, ln, sl	mus*cl*e, *l*ike, peo*pl*e, a*ll*, ki*ln*, i*sl*and

TABLE 3. Consonant Phonemes and Their Most Frequent Spellings (Continued)

	Phoneme	Graphemes	Examples
10.	/m/	lm, m, ½m, mb, mm, mn	palm, from, criticism, lamb, common, hymn
11.	/n/	gn, ½gn, kn, mn, mp, n, ½n, nd, nn, pn	gnaw, vignette, knows, mnemonic, comptroller, in, canon, handsome, dinner, pneumatic
12.	/ŋ/	n, nd, ng	think, handkerchief, thing
13.	/p/	p, ph, pp	pay, naphtha, happy
14.	/r/	l, r, re, rh, rps, rr, rrh, rt, wr	colonel, for, they're, rhyme, corps, carry, myrrh, mortgage, write
15.	/s/	c, ps, s, sc, sch, ss, st, sth, sw, tsw, ½x, z	cent, psalm, this, scene, schism, less, listen, isthmus, sword, boatswain, next, waltz
16.	/ʃh/	c, ce, ch, schi, ci, psh, s, sc, sch, sci, se, sh, si, ss, ssi, t, ti, ½x, ½xi	oceanic, ocean, chaise, fuschia, social, pshaw, sure, crescendo, schwa, conscience, nauseous, she, pension, issue, mission, negotiate, nation, luxury, noxious
17.	/t/	bt, cht, ct, ed, pt, t, th, tt, tw,	debt, yacht, indict, asked, receipt, it, thyme, little, two
18.	/þh/	th	thing
19.	/ðh/	th	that
20.	/v/	f, lv, v, ve, zv	of, halve, view, we've, rendezvous
21.	/w/	o, ½o-e, ou, u, w, ½wh	choir, one, bivouac, quite, wagon, when
22.	/y/	e, ½gu, i, j, ll, y	azalea, vignette, union, hallelujah, tortilla, yet
23.	/z/	cz, is, sc, si, sp, ss, sth, thes, x, ½x, z, zz	czar, is, discern, business, raspberry, scissors, asthma, clothes, xylophone, exact, zone, puzzle
24.	/ʒ/	g, s, si, ssi, ti, ½x, z, zi	rouge, pleasure, occasion, scission, equation, luxurious, azure, brazier

*The use of ½ preceding the graphemes in this table indicates that the grapheme represents more than one sound. In the case of x in *example* the x represents both /g/ and /z/.

uses 26 graphemes to represent its 20 consonant phonemes (roughly 77 percent phonetic), with an average of 1.3 graphemes per phoneme. In Italian, only one phoneme, /k/, is represented by 3 graphemes, *c, ch, q,* whereas 5 others are represented by 2 graphemes each, but only *z, c,* and *g* represent two different consonant phonemes. English is several times more difficult to learn to spell than Italian so far as its consonants are concerned, though the consonant phoneme-grapheme correspondences of English are considered more regular—that is, more phonetic—than its vowels.

The child's total task in learning to read (at this point thought of as decoding print to sound in the acquisition stage) could be immensely simplified by a reform in English orthography. However, given the situation as it stands now, the teacher's task is to combine a variety of techniques to help children learn to decode the complex of spelling patterns. The generalized procedures presented in Chapter 5, along with specific activities provided in subsequent chapters, introduce relevant methods for an attack on the problem.

INTRODUCING CONSONANTS

Let us now examine the procedures used in sequencing consonants in an instructional system, that is, the order in which they are introduced. Since letters are formed from lines, circles, and parts of circles, writing programs often begin with line letters such as *i* and *t;* next add the circle letter, *o;* and then develop the combination letters, *a, b, p,* and so on. This method assists children in developing a command of manuscript writing but it does not provide for a transition from language-experience records, where such print is used to record the experiences of children using their language and used for initial reading instruction, to reading book print. The use of manuscript writing was originally proposed to aid such a transition. As will be seen in Chapter 5, reactive inhibition in learning is created when different stimuli are used to represent a sound already known. This suggests that a decoding program might be best begun using only lower-case letters and then only with forms that are similar if not identical to those found in the target material, namely, books. Programs of writing should be used to support and reinforce decoding programs, but often they have been at variance with them; for example, the letter *a,* does not appear in printed material as it does in manuscript.

Although the use of this type of manuscript writing reflects a rigidity characteristic of the first half of this century, it is still prevalent in recent "perceptual development" materials. In *ABC and me*, for example, the word *b a l l o o n s* is used for the purpose of reinforcing letter discrimination by tracing the manuscript letter and is followed by the print version of balloons, which contains a dissimilar form of *a*. The materials of Clymer and Barrett (1969), Reading 360 Series, also use the same pattern dissimilarity in the name of perceptual development. However, the child will rarely if ever see the manuscript letter *a* in print, and this suggests that little concern is shown for transfer values of the materials used. When confronted with such dissimilarities, the teacher should act as an editor, correcting the material so as to prevent transfer difficulty. The teacher should also show the formation of the alternate form of *a*, that which is typically found in print, so that the upper- and two lower-case forms are introduced and "perceived." Materials such as the *Palo Alto Reading Series* show the alternative, as a matter of course. In Chapter 5, material is provided that can be used to correct inconsistencies and to ensure that transfer to print occurs.

Although the evidence from the Dewey, Mazurkiewicz, and Tanyzer (1963) and the Coleman (1972) studies points to a rational approach for sequencing graphemes, earlier usages are still in vogue. Studies with adults on the legibility of letters (Anderson and Dearborn, 1952) led to the acceptance of various sequences prevalent in most pre − 1960 basal materials. The assumption was made that if adults recognize consonants most easily at the beginning and end of target words flashed at 1/100 of a second, then children should be introduced to consonants first and certain consonants should have priority over others.

Obviously, the child learning to read is wholly unlike the adult who already knows how to read and who is familiar with printed symbols. Unfortunately, rather than working to determine how children learn to write and to recognize and learn associations of symbols with sounds they already know, researchers have developed materials, often in common use, that continue to use a sequence based on adult behavior, presumably on the assumption that children are little adults. Teachers should be wary of such approaches and should reject them in favor of a view such as that of Gates (1947), who indicated that teachers should teach children the letters they can learn most easily. This contrasts with opinions of others who stress that easily confused graphemes such as *b* and *d* or *p* and *q* should not be taught in close proximity. Yet research on training to discriminate among features of letters points to procedures that might be followed to avoid confusing one letter with another. The research of Gibson (1970), for example, demonstrates that the use of confusible letters in contrasting pairs provides the basis for the child to learn the distinctive features of each and to avoid misreading *d* for *b*, *p* for *d* or *g*, and so on.

The approach of Dewey, Mazurkiewicz, and Tanyzer (1963), characteristic of the *Early to Read* (1963) and Research Council of America (1964) i.t.a. programs, sequences vowels and consonants according to the frequency of sound occurrence in English and their utility in decoding and encoding. These two sets of materials originally followed the same sequence: *a, n, t, e, b, s, r, i, d, l,* and so on. This sequence of letters reflected research related to children's materials and represented a modification of Dewey's (1923) original research on adult materials. The complete sequence of letters, as noted in Table 4, shows the sequence of the thirty-nine phonemes of English and the letters used to represent them as taught in one reading series (Mazurkiewicz and Tanyzer, 1963); the sequence indicates a procedure that ordinarily might also be followed in traditional orthography.

Another way of sequencing the consonant and vowel letters is indicated by the work of Coleman (1972) and Bridge (1968). These researchers studied the ease with which naive five-year-old children learn to make thirty-five letter-sound associations. Table 5 indicates the sequence of learnability of grapheme-phoneme correspondences. When the data were regrouped, Coleman and Bridge

TABLE 4. Sequence of Thirty-nine Phonemes, Based on Frequency of Sound Occurrence

1. /a/	14. /o/	27. /au/
2. /n/	15. /m/	28. /ŋ/
3. /t/	16. /k/	29. /ʃh/
4. /e/	17. /v/	30. /w/
5. /b/	18. /p/	31. /g/
6. /s/	19. /æ/	32. /y/
7. /r/	20. /ɛɛ/	33. /ou/
8. /i/	21. /f/	34. /ch/
9. /d/	22. /w/	35. /j/
10. /l/	23. /u/	36. /th/
11. /ɟh/	24. /ɷ/	37. /ue/
12. /œ/	25. /ie/	38. /oi/
13. /z/	26. /n/	39. /ʒ/

TABLE 5. Sequence of Ease of Learning of Grapheme-Phoneme Associations

Grapheme	Phoneme	Example
1. s	/s/	Santa
2. i-e	/ie/	tie
3. o-e	/œ/	toe
4. z	/z/	zebra
5. sh	/ʃh/	shoe
6. o	/o/	ostrich
7. ow	/ɑu/	how
8. m	/m/	monkey
9. u-e	/yɷ/	due
10. k	/k/	key
11. oo	/ɷ/	boot
12. f	/f/	fish
13. th	/ʤh/	feather
14. v	/v/	valentine
15. e-e	/ɛ/	tree
16. a-e	/æ/	cake
17. p	/p/	pencil
18. ch	/ʤh/	chair
19. b	/b/	bell
20. j	/j/	jack-o-lantern
21. r	/r/	rabbit
22. l	/l/	lion
23. g	/g/	goat
24. oy	/ɔi/	boy
25. n	/n/	nest
26. a	/a/	apple
27. aw	/ɑu/	law
28. w	/w/	wagon
29. d	/d/	dog
30. h	/h/	have
31. t	/t/	table
32. e	/e/	Eskimo
33. y	/y/	yo-yo
34. u	/u/	sun
35. i	/i/	Indian

independently found that sibilant consonants (s, z, sh) were learned with the most ease and short vowels with the most difficulty. A sequence in phonic materials of easily learned consonants and long vowels would be more appropriate than one of consonants and short vowels in traditional print, as opposed to the sequence possible in a reformed orthography such as i.t.a. This rationale can be tempered by the teacher to include consonant-vowel sequences that both appear with high frequency in printed materials and are familiar to children or are present in their speech, since the difference in learnability of graphemes in the table was demonstrated often to be as little as .06.

ALL ABOUT CONSONANTS

As can be seen in Table 3, the consonant phonemes /b/, /d/, /g/, /h/, /ʒ/, /p/, /ᵭh/, and /ʮh/ are represented by the fewest graphemes, whereas the letters *b, d, h, m, p,* and *r* each represent only one phoneme, though *m* and *h* are often used in combination with another consonant to represent additional phonemes. As seen in Table 6, *m*

TABLE 6. Most Frequent Graphemes for the Twenty-four Consonant Phonemes

Phoneme	Graphemes in Order of Frequency
1. /b/	b, bb
2. /ʧh/	ch, t, tch, ti
3. /d/	d, dd
4. /f/	f, ph, ff
5. /g/	g, gg, x
6. /h/	h, wh
7. /j/	g, j, dg
8. /k/	c, k, ct, ch
9. /l/	l, ll
10. /m/	m, mm
11. /n/	n, nn
12. /p/	p, pp
13. /r/	r, rr
14. /s/	s, c, ss
15. /ʃh/	ti, sh, ci, ssi, si, c, sh, t, s
16. /t/	t, tt
17. /ᵭh/	th
18. /ʮh/	th
19. /v/	v
20. /w/	w, u
21. /y/	i, y
22. /z/	s, z, es, x, zz, ss
23. /ʒ/	si, s, g, z
24. /ŋ/	ng, n

is tenth in the sequence of learnability, whereas the others are usually more difficult to learn. Although some authors would suggest that teaching phonics might be easier if begun using these six letters that represent only one sound each, learnability and utility in decoding are of far greater importance.

Accepting the results of the Hanna et al. (1966) study, which reported the most frequent spellings for the consonant phonemes, but reducing the number of phonemes from their thirty to the twenty-four significant consonant phonemes necessary to teach children, one can see that the information in Table 6 might be of some value in teaching spelling or encoding of sound, particularly if syllable positions and stress rules are added in the instruction. However, grapheme-to-phoneme correspondence is the only concern in teaching phonics, or decoding. In Table 7 the relevant information is reordered to recognize this concern. Table 7 shows that the graphemes *b, k, m, p, q, r, v,* and *w* represent one phoneme and, where the phonemes are separated by a semicolon, that *f, h, j,* and *l* represent a second phoneme very infrequently. For example, *f*

TABLE 7. Grapheme-to-Phoneme Maps

Grapheme	Phonemes in Order of Frequency
b	/b/
c	/k/, /s/; /ʃh/
d	/d/, /t/; /j/
f	/f/; /v/
g	/g/, /j/; /ʒ/
h	/h/; /țh/
j	/j/; /y/
k	/k/
l	/l/; /r/
m	/m/
n	/n/, /ŋ/
p	/p/
q	/k/
r	/r/
s	/s/, /z/, /ʒ/, /ʃh/
t	/t/, /ɖh/, /ʃh/
v	/v/
w	/w/
x	/ks/, /kz/; /k/, /z/
y	/ɛɛ/, /y/, /ie/; /u/
z	/z/; /s/, /ʒ/

represents /f/ in *fun, father, for,* and *feel* but /v/ only in *of.* If you teach children the special use of *f* for /v/ in *of* as you help them to identify *of* as a sight word, *f* can be treated as though it represented only one phoneme.

Since *b, k, m, p, q, r, v, w* and *f* represent the sounds normally heard in the initial position of *bell, key, man, pen, queen, rabbit, vase, wagon,* and *father,* there is no need to discuss them further. Doubled, or *geminate,* consonants represent the same phoneme as the single consonant as seen and heard in such word pairs as *rub-rubber, sum-summer, dip-dipper, war-warrior,* and *off-if.* The letter *j* may be treated briefly since it normally represents the sound heard in the initial position of *jump* and only rarely, as in *hallelujah,* represents the /y/ sound. Since this word is a loan word from German, which typically uses the *j* to represent /y/, its pronunciation irregularity can be understood. On the other hand, *h* has some interesting uses as a diacritic.

DIACRITIC DEFINED

Diacritic marks such as ¯, ˘, ˆ, and so on are familiar to most users of dictionaries. They are orthographic marks indicating a phonetic value different from that given an unmarked character. Letters, too, have been identified as diacritics (Gove, 1966: 622). The use of the letter *e* as a graphical device apparently came into use early in the development of our irregular spelling system. Its first use might well have been after the character *v* to distinguish between that character's use to represent the /v/ in *very* and the /u/ in *bvt* when the *v* was used to represent /v/, /w/, and /u/. Since the final *e* was pronounced in Middle English, such possible graphical usages are often conjectural. We do know, however, that *vv,* in time, came to represent /w/ to distinguish between the sounds *v* represented. Similarly, it is thought that *e* after *v* at the end of words was used to denote the /v/ sound. Whether this view of the development of our spelling system is correct or not, the usage of *e* as a diacritic is generally accepted among students of the orthography.

The diacritic, therefore, is defined as a letter or mark which is used to denote graphic information of phonetic value. The diacritic letter has two usages, graphical and relational. Following the letter *v* in *sleeve, believe, give,* or *have,* the diacritic *e* has a graphical usage to indicate that the letter *v* is almost never word-final (the last letter in a printed word), whereas after *i* or *o* in such words as *tie, lie, toe,* and *shoe,* it has a relational value indicating that the adjacent vowel has its name sound. The generalization below shows that the diacritic *e* has at least eleven such usages.

Primary Generalization

GENERALIZATION: The *e* at the end of words is a diacritic that signals a change from the expected in the preceding consonantal or vocalic.

As shown by Mazurkiewicz (1974), this generalization accounts for over 92 percent of the usages of *e* at the end of words. Only rarely does the *e* at the end of words represent a phoneme. In fact, it represented the phoneme /εε/ in only thirteen words in the Rinsland corpus: *adobe, algae, apostrophe, coyote, recipe, ukelele, be, he, me, she, we, ye,* and *the* when accented. In *cafe* and *coupe,* both from French, the phoneme represented is /æ/, and in *the, e* represents /u/, /i/, or /εε/, depending on whether the following word contains an initial consonant or vowel, or whether it is stressed or unstressed.

GENERALIZATION: If the only vowel letter is at the end of a onesyllable word, the letter usually stands for a long sound.

The words *be, he, me, she, we,* and *ye* can be accounted for using the above generalization. *Adobe, algae, apostrophe,* and *ukelele,* as well as *cafe* and *coupe,* can be related to their Spanish, Greek, or French origins. *Coyote,* having two pronunciations, /k ɪe œ t εε/ and /k ɪe œ t/, may be taught in either form and *recipe* can be taught as an exception to the fact that final *e* is usually silent and even related to the period in linguistic history when final *e*'s were generally inflected. Instruction related to these eight words, of course, would not ordinarily occur in the primary years, since the words do not often appear in children's materials. But when they do occur, these procedures could be used.

Secondary Generalizations as Related to Consonants

GENERALIZATION: The *e* following *v* at the end of a word is silent and indicates that *v* almost never comes at the end of a word.

Only one exception to this generalization, *Slav*, has been found, and this can be shown to relate to Yugoslavia or to Slavic people. The convention in spelling of placing an *e* after *v* to indicate that *v* is never word final has held to this date. It is not only of value in teaching decoding but also encoding since the child can be taught that, except for the words *of* and *Slav*, whenever he or she hears a /v/ at the end of a word, an *e* should be added. The use of this rule is beneficial in reading too since the child should not ordinarily have difficulty in recognizing such words as *give* or *have* because the vowels in these words are unglided or short when the *e* after *v* rule is applied first.

GENERALIZATION: The *e* following *z* at the end of a word is silent and indicates that *z* almost never comes at the end of a word.

Like *v*, *z* in primary-level materials would have 100 percent utility. At later levels, such words as *quiz*, *whiz*, and *fizz* may occur; thus, the rule includes the words "almost never." Although it can be shown that Middle English writers used *zz* to end words spelled with a *z* and that *quiz*, *fizz*, and *whiz* are fairly recent back formations (i.e., words formed by dropping the last part of a word) from *quizzical*, *fizzle*, and *wizard*, the rule is of value to decoding and encoding.

A combination of these two generalizations reduces the number of rules a child might need to learn, since they can be restated as follows:

GENERALIZATION: The *e* following *v* and *z* at the end of words is silent and indicates that *v* and *z* almost never come at the end of a word.

Generalizations related to *c* and *g* may similarly be combined to form a generalization accounting for both.

GENERALIZATION: The *e* following *c* and *g* at the end of words is silent and indicates that *c* is pronounced /s/ as in *Santa* and *g* is pronounced /j/ as in *giant*.

In the case of *c*, the rule has 100 percent utility, and in the case of *g*, almost 94 percent utility. Such *ge*-ending words as *fusilage*, *garage*, and *rouge* might be found in elementary-level materials, and the *g* pronounced as either /j/ or /ʒ/. Although both are correct pronunciations and no attempt to change these is suggested, in areas where the *g* is pronounced /j/ the rule would have universal applicability. In other areas, and even within the same classroom, the two different sounds will occur, and teachers should be prepared to explain that the rule doesn't always apply because of different pronunciations among different people.

GENERALIZATION: The *e* following *th* at the end of a word indicates that the *th* is pronounced /ᵭh/ as in *breathe*.

This rule has 100 percent utility and may be demonstrated to a class by listing words such as *breath, teeth, wreath*, and *bath*, having the children supply the pronunciations, and then adding the final *e* to show that the sound represented by *th* changes to /ᵭh/ when the *e* is added.

GENERALIZATION: The *e* following *ng* at the end of a word indicates that the *ng* is pronounced /n/ and /j/.

A listing of *lung, sing*, and *bring* should be followed by the addition of *e* to each word to show that the *n* and *g* now represent the /n/, *nest*, and /j/, *giant*, sounds. This rule has 100 percent utility.

GENERALIZATION: The *e* following a consonant plus *l* at the end of words indicates that *l* is pronounced /ul/.

In the case of such words as *able, table, circle, turtle, cradle*, and the like, the *e* indicates that the *l* is syllabic, that it should be recognized as representing a reduced or unstressed /u/ and the /l/. The syllables *ble, cle, dle, tle* can be written as *bul, cul, dul, tul*, respectively, to show this phonetic pronunciation. But the pronunciation might also be described to children as though the *bl* and *cl* were in the initial position of words like *block* or *clock*. The object here is to eliminate pronunciations like /a-pul/ and /tæ-bul/, where each syllable is stressed. The variety of consonant plus *le* patterns to which the rule applies is extensive *(ble, cle, dle, fle, gle, ple, xle, zle)*. However, the words *whistle, wrestle*, and *thistle* contain a silent *t* remaining from Middle English pronunciation, which contrasts with the pronounced *t* of *turtle* or *hurtle*. Although the *le* rule applies, special mention of the silent *t* in *whistle, wrestle*, and *thistle* must be made to children.

Other exceptions are few, since this rule has 98 percent utility. The exceptions *isle* and *aisle* can be taught as such or as sight words, whereas *vaudeville* and *mademoiselle,* where *lle* appears, can be taught in either of two ways—as exceptions because they are French loan words, or as exceptions because the rule doesn't apply to *ll* situations.

The *e* following *r* in *fire, hire, tire, acre,* and *massacre* is recognized as having the same function as *e* following *l.* It, too, indicates that the *r* is syllabic and is pronounced /ur/. Again the /u/ is a reduced sound. This function explains why many children have difficulty in accepting that *hire, tire,* and *fire* are one-syllable words and why they often misspell these words, adding the letter *u* before *r* in their spellings, giving *tiur* and *fiur.* However, this usage of *e* after *r* is minor and is not included in the generalization. A discussion of it, if presented at all, should be deferred until the *e* after *l* generalization is mastered.

GENERALIZATION: The *e* following *s* at the end of words indicates that the *s* is pronounced as either /s/ or /z/; try the /z/ sound first.

This generalization has 100 percent utility, but the /z/ sound is the more frequent one. There is no way of predicting the sound short of trying each one in turn.

GENERALIZATION: The *e* in *dure, ture, sure,* and *zure* endings of words indicates that the *d, t, s,* and *z* are pronounced /j/, /ch/, /sh/, and /z/, respectively.

This generalization has 98 percent utility since only one exception, *endure,* was found. In each case, the vowel plus *r* might be thought of as either a phonemic cluster, a diphthong, or a glided sound since *ur* represents /ur/. However, there is no reason to do so since the *u* and *r* represent their regular sounds with *u* sounded as /u/.

Secondary generalizations as applied to vowels will be discussed in Chapter 4 to avoid repetition.

GENERALIZATIONS ABOUT CONSONANTS

Research into the utility of generalizations about consonants found in reading instruction materials in the years before 1963 was initiated by Clymer (1963). His findings, supported by Bailey (1967) and Emans (1967), indicate both the value and inadequacy of several generalizations in instruction. Clymer's criterion was that the

TABLE 8. Generalizations About Consonants

Generalization	Clymer	Bailey	Emans
1. When *c* and *h* are next to each other, they make only one sound.	100#	100#	100#
2. *Ch* is usually pronounced as it is in *kitchen, catch,* and *chair,* not like *sh.*	95#	87	67
3. When *c* is followed by *e* or *i,* the sound of *s* is likely to be heard.	96#	92#	90#
4. When the letter *c* is followed by *o* or *a,* the sound of *k* is likely to be heard.	100#	100#	100#
5. The letter *g* often has a sound similar to that of *j* in *jump* when it precedes the letters *i* or *e.*	64	78	80#
6. When *ght* is seen in a word, *gh* is silent.	100#	100	100
7. When a word begins *kn,* the *k* is silent.	100	100	100
8. When a word begins with *wr,* the *w* is silent.	100	100	100
9. When two of the same consonants are side by side, only one is heard.	99#	98#	91#
10. When a word ends in *ck,* it has the same last sound as in *look.*	100#	100	100

#Indicates in each study when the generalization was found to be of value.

generalization be applicable to at least twenty words with 75 percent accuracy. A comparison of the findings of Clymer, Bailey, and Emans is presented in Table 8. Although Clymer found several consonant generalizations of value, it can be seen that generalizations 2, 6, 7, 8, and 10 did not always meet the criterion of value since they did not appear often enough to merit teaching when different samples of words were used. Since the three studies presented in Table 8 differ markedly in the word samples chosen, it is difficult to go beyond this statement. Specific discussion of these studies will appear in Chapter 5, since most of the rules they studied refer to vowels. Reference to the generalizations in Table 8 or modifications of them will be made as they apply to the consonant letters in sequence.

THE INDIVIDUAL CONSONANT GRAPHEMES

c

When the letter *c* is used by itself, Table 7 shows that it has normally two pronunciations, that of the /k/ in *cat* and /s/ in *city*.

GENERALIZATION: When *c* is followed by *e*, *i*, or *y*, the sound of *s* in *sat* is usually heard; when it is followed by *o*, *a*, or *u*, the sound of *k* in *keep* is usually heard.

The research of Clymer, Bailey, Emans, and others relates only partially to this generalization, since *y* was not included in the generalizations studied by any of the researchers.

Eliminating *y* from consideration, the two generalizations, *c* sounded as /s/ and as /k/, have at least 90 percent and 100 percent utility respectively. But by adding *y* to the first part of the generalization, its overall value is increased and it is found to be especially useful.

Some authors prefer to refer to the /s/ and /k/ sounds of *c* as soft and hard, respectively. In the above generalization, however, these terms are eliminated in favor of an example, since simplification of instruction for children is the hallmark of good pedagogy. To ask children to learn the use of the terms *hard* and *soft* is to request them to master a higher level of abstraction to identify sounds merely because the terms are used in phonetics. Referring to key words or to words in children's vocabulary enhances their learning while eliminating extraneous terminology. If the child sees the word *candy* and follows the usual generalization, he or she might say "*c* before *a* is a hard *c* sound that's like the *k* in *key*," when, in fact, his or her reasoning can be simplified to "*c* before *a* is like the *k* in *key*."

The rule concerning geminate consonants that states "two like letters are pronounced as one" would ordinarily apply to such words as *occupy* or *tobacco*, even though in writing we would break the word between the double consonants. In contrast, the geminate consonant *cc* before *e* or *i* in multisyllable words represents two different phonemes, /k/ and /s/, as seen in the words *success*, /sukses/, and *accident*, /aksident/. Because there are few examples *(soccer)* to refute these usages, a secondary generalization related to *cc* might be taught.

GENERALIZATION: Double *c* before *u* and *o* usually sounds like the *k* in *key*. Double *c* before *e* and *i* usually represents two sounds, the /k/ in *key* and /s/ in *sat*.

When *c* stands before *i* and *e* in such words as *conscious, special, ancient, ocean, official, social, delicious,* and *racial* (see p. 40, the diacritic *i*), it represents the phoneme /ʃh/ in 1 to 10 percent of the words used in various word corpuses.

Although the *i* can be considered morphophonemic since it is silent in *special* /speʃhull/ but pronounced in *speciality* /speʃheeali-tee/, it might be better to teach it as one of several diacritic letters that act in unstressed syllables before another vowel to signal a change from the expected pronunciation of /s/. The procedure used by some teachers to indicate that *sci* and *ci* before another vowel represent /ʃh/ accounts for little more than half the occurrences, whereas the diacritic or morphophonemic identification of *i* before *c* (as well as *s, t, z*) recognizes its double usages in the simple and derived forms of additional words. The best procedure might be to follow the generalization that "*c* before *i* or *e* and another vowel letter is usually pronounced /ʃh/, and the *i* and *e* are usually silent." The addition of *e* to the generalization accounts for the sound in the word *ocean*. (See also *h*, p. 50, for information about *c* followed by *h*, as in *church* and *chew*.)

Exceptions to c as /k/ or /s/

In American pronunciation, there are only a few exceptions to the generalizations given above. Nonetheless, it should be noted that *sc* in *crescendo* and in one pronunciation of *fascist* represents the /ʃh/ phoneme, whereas the typical pattern of *sc* representing /s/ is seen in the words *scene* and *science*. The /ʤh/ pronunciation of *c* is reserved for a small number of Italian or Slavic loan words: *concerto, cello, duce*. The unusual pronunciation of *cz* as /s/ or /ʤh/ is reserved for loan words from Slavic nations: *Czar, Czechoslovakia*. The *cz* spelling of *eczema*, however, represents /kz/. In addition, Americans pronounce *Celts* as /selts/ rather than /kelts/, as do the British. In this case, the generalization of "*c* before *e, i,* and *y*," and so on seems to have overcome the earlier pronunciation.

d

There are two regular pronunciations of *d*, /d/ and /t/, and one unusual pronunciation, /j/ as in *educator* /ejukætor/, with the most frequent pronunciation being /d/ as in *dog*. The geminate consonants, *dd*, have the same pronunciation as the single *d*. The /t/ pronunciation is found in the morpheme *ed*, which has the relational meaning of past tense. The three pronunciations of *ed*, /ed/, /d/, and /t/, are for the most part unpredictable, since suggesting that *ed* is pronounced /t/ after voiceless consonants (except *t*), as some authors do, is found to be inconsistent. For example, *watch-watched* have a /t/ pronunciation, but *wretch-wretched* have an /ed/ sound. It is more desirable, therefore, to teach the alternative pronunciations directly.

The /j/ sound of *d* appears to be related only to the word *educate* and its derivatives and therefore can be taught when this group of words occur.

g

As indicated in Table 7, the letter *g* has two frequently used pronunciations, /g/ as in *goat* and /j/ as in *gem*, and one less frequently used pronunciation, /ʒ/. The latter occurs chiefly in French loan words such as *garage* or *rouge*, which, in American speech, are often but not always pronounced /j/.

GENERALIZATION: *g* before *e*, *i*, and *y* usually sounds like /j/ in *jump*; before *o*, *a*, and *u*, it usually sounds like /g/ in *goat*.

Burmeister (1968) reports this generalization to be especially useful, but the research of Clymer, Bailey, and Emans indicates that the first half of the generalization has a utility from as little as 64 percent to as high as 80 percent.

The usage of the /j/ sound of *g* holds up well in medial position of words *(magic, agent)* and before *e* at the end of words *(age, large)*, but *g* before *e*, *i*, and *y* in the initial position may also represent /g/ *(get, gem, give, giant)* in at least 20 percent of its occurrences. Although only a few words are involved, the lack of predictability requires that a child be flexible in knowing the two pronunciations.

The diacritic *e* generalization for *g* followed by *e* at the end of words is of value in helping reduce uncertainty about which pronunciation *g* has in this position. This generalization states that "the *e* following a *g* at the end of a word indicates that *g* is pronounced as /j/" and was found to have some 96 percent utility (Mazurkiewicz, 1974). In areas of the United States where such words as *fuselage*, *garage*, and *rouge* are pronounced to rhyme with *college*, the rule would have almost universal application. Since both pronunciations are correct and the /j/ sound has supplanted the /ʒ/ sound of *g* in these positions in many words, there is little reason to enforce the /ʒ/ pronunciation.

Similarly, the diacritic *e* generalization that states that *e* after *ng* at the end of words indicates that *n* and *g* are pronounced /n/ and /j/ is of interest here, since the generalization was found to have 100 percent utility (Mazurkiewicz, 1974).

When the *g* is found as a geminate (for instance, *piggy*, *buggy*, *rugged*), its usage is almost always as /g/, the exceptions being *exaggerate* and *suggest*. In combination with other letters (*gh, gn, gu,* and *ng*), *g* has a range of usages that are discussed below (see *h, n,* and diacritic *e*).

h

The letter *h* represents the consonant sound heard in the initial position of *hat* and is pronounced only when it occurs before vowels. It also may be silent and act as a diacritic in a large number of words.

1. Initial *h* is always silent in *heir, honest, honor* and *hour* and in their derivatives *heiress, honesty, honorable, hourly.* Silent *h* is the more frequent usage in the word *herb* but not in its derivatives, *herbaceous, herbivorous,* and *herbal.* While pronunciations of *herb* /urb, hurb/ appear to be moving more toward the pronounced *h*, in agreement with its derivatives, the word *humble* retains its *h* as the most frequent American pronunciation. A child, knowing the sound associated with *h*, will probably want to decode the word *herb* with an initial *h* sound. A teacher would be correct, in the task of simplifying the decoding activities, to maintain consistency in the pronunciation of *herb* and *herbivorous,* and to opt for the pronounced *h*.

2. *h* is always silent in the combinations *kh* and *rh: khaki, khan, rhyme, rhythm, myrrh, Rhine,* and so on.

3. *h* is usually silent in the combination *exh* as in *exhaust, exhibit,* and their derivatives but not in *exhale* or *exhume.*

4. The *h* is usually silent between a consonant and a following unstressed vowel, as in *shepherd* and *silhouette;* but the word *per-*

haps always retains the pronounced *h* and the word *forehead* does the same more often than not.

As a diacritic, *h* is also silent when it occurs after a vowel in the final position of a word and following *c, g, p, s, t,* and *w.*

1. When *h* occurs in the final position of words after *a, e,* or *o* as in *ah, bah, hurrah, eh,* and *oh,* it is often described as a vowel since it is said to form a combination with the vowels to represent certain vowel sounds. In a study of the occurrence of these words in the Rinsland *Basic Vocabulary* (1945) and the Harris and Jacobson *Basic Elementary Reading Vocabularies* (1972), only the words *ah,* b*ah,* hurr*ah,* raj*ah, eh,* ok*eh* (as a variant spelling for *okey, okay*), and *oh* appear in either corpus through the eighth-reader level. Other words that come to mind include *Shiloh, Shenandoah,* and *hallelujah.*

Although the practice of describing *h* as a vowel is given above, the teacher should avoid the temptation of extending the description of the vowel letters to "*a, e, i, o,* and sometimes *h, w, y,* and *u.*" The teacher should describe the *h* as a diacritic, which indicates that the vowel letter represents a sound different from the expected. After *a,* it indicates the broad sound of *a* as in *car;* after *e,* the sound of *a* in *angel;* and after *o,* the sound of the letter name.

The alternative of teaching the words as sight words would appear to be permissible in respect to *ah* and *oh* only in beginning reading, but even here procedures that encourage children to form their own generalizations or those that provide them with decoding tools which would make them more independent in word recognition would be more advantageous.

2. *h* as a diacritic, however, is seen in its ubiquitous role in the combinations *ch, gh, ph, sh, th,* and *wh.* In the Rinsland vocabulary list, 1,771 instances of *h* in combination with a consonant were identified in 1,737 words out of the 14,571 entries in the corpus; thus, almost 12 percent of this vocabulary contains words in which the diacritic *h* can be applied. Of the 1,771 consonant plus *h* combinations in the 1,737 words there were:

531 words containing *ch* with 3 pronunciations—/ʧh/, /k/, /ʃh/— and silent

431 words containing *th* with 2 pronunciations: /ʧh/, /ʤh/

407 words containing *sh* with 1 pronunciation: /ʃh/

197 words containing *gh* with 2 pronunciations—/f/, /g/—and silent

98 words containing *ph* with 1 pronunciation: /f/
85 words containing *wh* with 2 pronunciations: /wh/, /h/

Based on this list, generalizations could be made that would generally have utilities of 100 percent. For example,

1. The diacritic *h* after *c* indicates that the *c* may be silent or pronounced /ȼh/, /k/, and /ʃh/; try the /ȼh/ sound first.
2. The diacritic *h* after *t* indicates that the *t* may be pronounced as either /țh/ or /ᵭh/; try the /țh/ sound first (the one exception is *thyme* /tiem/).
3. The diacritic *h* after *s* indicates that the *s* is always pronounced /ʃh/.
4. The diacritic *h* after *g* indicates that the *g* is usually silent, but that in a few words it represents the sounds /f/ or /g/.
5. The diacritic *h* after *p* indicates that the *p* is pronounced /f/.
6. The diacritic *h* after *w* indicates that the *w* and *h* may be pronounced /h/ and /w/, or that the *h* is pronounced and the *w* is silent.

Of these, generalizations 3 and 5 are most satisfactory since each refers to only one sound, and any child applying them to words such as *should, shall, bush, rash, phone, photo,* or *phonics* could readily decode these letter units.

A child using generalization 1 and trying to decode *ache* would first arrive at /æ ȼh/ and then at /æ k/. If the child is confronted with *mustache,* he or she would ordinarily try /mustaȼh/ and /mustak/ before achieving the right pronunciation. In fact, short of memorizing each word, there are no better alternatives available, since it is not possible to lay down any hard and fast rules to predict the pronunciation of *ch* except before consonants, where it is always pronounced /k/. All three pronunciations are found in initial, medial, and final positions, whereas silent *ch* is found in only one word: *yacht.*

1. /ȼh/ as in *chair* is the most common of the pronunciations (89 percent). Phonetically, this supposed sound is really two sounds and, by definition, is classified as a diphthong. Phonetically, the /ȼh/ sound cluster is written /tʃh/; in the respelling of /matȼh/, for instance, the *t* is redundant since the /t/ sound is included in the sounds represented by the character /ȼh/. The sound /ȼh/ is found mainly in words of Anglo-Saxon or early Latin or French origin. After short stressed vowels we frequently find the spelling *tch* instead of *ch.*

Examples of words of Anglo-Saxon origin include *chap, cheap, chin, cheek, cheese, chest, chew, chicken, child, choose, church, each, reach, teach, speech, rich, which, much, such, itch, watch, arch, starch, birch, orchard.*

Examples of words of French, Bantu or Sanskrit origins include *chance, change, chapter, chase, chair, check, chief, chimpanzee, Chinese, chocolate, peach, brooch, couch, touch, catch, pinch, march.*

2. /ʃh/ as in ma*ch*ine is mainly found in French loan words but also from other sources. Examples of the /ʃh/ sound include *chalet, chamois, chauffeur, chef, machine, parachute, sachet, cliché, chic, Chevrolet, Michigan, Chicago.*

3. /k/, as in *Christmas*, is usually found in loan words of Greek origin. Examples of the /k/ sound of *ch* before consonants also include *chlorine, chrome, Chrysler, technique.* Before vowels, the /k/ sound of *ch* is found in *chaos, character, chemical, orchestra, architect, monarch, chorus, choir, anchor, echo,* and *stomach* (*ache* is of Anglo-Saxon origin).

4. The *t* before *ch* in *patch, pitch, watch, itch,* and *butcher* can be also said to act as a diacritic to indicate that *ch* is pronounced in these words as /ʃh/. The inadequacy of the alphabet to evoke the sounds of English that Middle English writers were attempting to deal with by using letters as diacritics is clearly seen in such cases.

Generalization 2 in Table 8 regarding the diacritic *h* presents a different problem. In a study of 100,000 running words (words in written discourse), Dewey (1923) found that the voiced *th* sound as in *father, the,* and *them* was the more frequently used of the two sounds of *th.* Although this finding may be due to the very frequent use of such words as *the, that,* and *this,* in written discourse, it is in direct contrast to the higher number of words that contain the voiceless /ʈh/ as compared to the voiced /ɟh/ sound. Almost 74 percent of the *th* words children wrote contained the voiceless /ʈh/ sound as in *thumb.*

Thus, a child confronted with a list of words, or words in isolation, should apply generalization 2 as given. However, since the child will only rarely need to apply decoding principles outside the context of written discourse (i.e., running words), we might want to modify "try the /ʈh/ sound first" to "try the /ɟh/ *(feather)* sound first." Nevertheless, because instruction in decoding is on isolated words and specific words in context, the temptation to modify the generalization should be resisted.

When the two *th* sounds are found in initial, medial, and final positions, there are some other ways to distinguish between them.

1. In a final position, except for the verb form of *mouth* and *smooth*, as well as *with* and a few others, the voiceless sound is usually found. *With* and *smooth*, while also pronounced with the voiceless /th̯/, are more frequently pronounced /wiðh/ and /smoõðh/, respectively. *Bath, birth, both, cloth, earth, eleventh, fifth, fourth, sixth, month, moth,* and *path* are examples of the voiceless *th* at the end of words. To simplify the child's task, the teacher might want to include *with* and *smooth* among the words that illustrate the voiceless *th* at the end of words. No particular harm will result in the case of *with* since there is no consistent general practice, but it should be noted that the voiced /ðh/ is the only pronunciation of smoo*th*ly given by dictionaries. A child would probably pronounce *smoothly* in the manner specified by the dictionary, but such a simplification might produce incorrect pronunciations. Thus, *smooth* is better left as an exception to the voiceless /th̯/ found in the final position of words, whereas *with* may be used in either of its pronounced forms according to local practice.

2. In the final position before the silent *e*, the *th* is always voiced. Examples: *bathe, breathe, sheathe, wreathe, teethe, clothe, soothe, scythe.*

3. In the initial position, *th* is voiceless except in the article *the*, in the pronouns *they, them, their, that, this, those, these* (also *thou, thee, thy*), and in the conjunctions and adverbs *than, this, there, though, although,* and *thus.* Examples of the voiceless /th̯/ in the initial position include *thing, thick, thin, thank, think, through, three,* and *thirty.* (*th* represents /t/ in only one word, *thyme*, in the initial position.)

4. In the medial position, short of knowing the origin of words, there is no way of predicting the correct sound and therefore reliance on the generalization should be promoted.

Generalization 4 regarding the diacritic *h* has 100 percent utility and applies to 196 of 1,771 instances of the consonant *g* followed by *h*, as shown in the list below:

175 words where the *gh* was silent: 89.3 percent
15 words where the *gh* represented /f/: 7.7 percent
6 words where the *gh* represented /g/: 3.1 percent

Since generalization 4 says essentially that *h* is silent and indicates *g* is mostly silent, it is best simply to list the words in which *gh* represents /g/ or /f/ and note that in all other words the *gh* is silent.

1. *gh* in an initial position never represents anything but the /g/ sound: *ghost, ghostly, ghastly, ghetto, gherkin.* George Bernard Shaw created the word *ghoti* to represent the word *fish* in an attempt at showing the irregularity of English spelling. But *ghoti* is itself inadequate since it does not follow the rule for the usage of *gh* in initial positions. *gh*, however, also represents the /g/ sound in the medial positions of a few words: *sorghum, spaghetti, burghers.*

2. The /f/ sound of *gh* is found in the final positions of words only when the *gh* is preceded by *au* or *ou*. Examples: *cough, enough, laugh, rough, trough.* As a further illustration, the modernized spelling of *draft* for *draught* should be encouraged. Since *gh* after *au* or *ou* in *caught, through, though,* and so on is silent, focusing learning on those words where the *gh* represents /f/ automatically makes all other usages silent.

Generalization 5 regarding the diacritic *h* has been found to have 100 percent utility, although some individuals pronounce the *ph* in di*ph*theria and di*ph*thong as a /p/ sound, probably as a result of the confusion generated by inadequate knowledge about the function of *ph*. *ph* has only one regular pronunciation and generally it occurs in words of Greek origin. It is used in initial, medial, and final positions.

Generalization 6 regarding the diacritic *h* accounts for all the instances of *wh* found in print and can be taught as stated. However, instruction with young children is more direct if the few words where only the sound of *h* is heard are given in the generalization. A restatement such as "the diacritic *h* after *w* indicates that the /h/ and /w/ sounds are pronounced except in the words *who, whom, whose, whole, whoop* and their derivatives, where only the /h/ sound is heard" clarifies the use of *h* here. *wh* is pronounced /h/ only before *o*. Since it appears that American speakers are increasingly equating *wh* with /w/, making no distinction between the beginning sounds in *weather* and *whether*, a generalization that states that "*h* after *w* indicates that /w/ is pronounced except in the words *who, whom*, and so on" would more realistically recognize this speech tendency while at the same time avoid the implication that the child who does not aspirate (begin a word with the /h/ sound) before *w* is using substandard speech. The use of the words *weather* and *whether* in a speech context always denotes their meanings even though the aspiration before *w* in *whether* is eliminated.

Although another version of the generalization could account for both the /h/ before /w/ and the /w/ pronunciations, teachers are encouraged to choose the generalization that reflects the dominant pronunciation in their areas and to avoid any implication of wrong speech among children in their classes where the alternate pronunciation exists.

l

The normal pronunciation of *l* or *ll* is the same as the phonetic value as found in the initial position of *lion, let,* or *loss* and the final position of *tall, bell,* or *fill.* The unusual pronunciation of *l* as /r/ appears in the word *colonel,* /kurnal/, which sometimes occurs in children's materials at the fourth-reader level.

n

The graphemes *n* or *nn* most frequently represent the sound heard at the beginning of the word *nest* and present little difficulty in learning so long as the features which *n* is composed of, line-arch-line, are identified.

However, *n* also represents /ŋ/ in a number of words, such as *thank,* /thaŋk/, *think, ink, Lincoln, finger, English, uncle, monkey, banquet, anger,* and *anxious.* "The letter *n* represents the /ŋ/ phoneme when it is followed by *c, k, q,* or *x*" might be developed as a rule. This is not a consistent usage when words like *pancake* or *pincushion* are examined, but since these words are compounds, little or no difficulty is experienced when only the general rule is taught to children following the early development of decoding skill with *pin* and *pan.*

Dictionary references show that *n* followed by *g* also represents the /ŋ/ sound in the respellings of /fiŋ-gur/ and /aŋ-gur/ and that each letter, *n* and *g,* represents a sound. In contrast, the derived forms of *long* and *sing,* /loŋ-gur/ and /siŋ-gur/, are not always indicated as containing a pronounced *g.* The rule can thus be further modified to state that "*n* represents /ŋ/ when followed by *c, k, q, x,* or *g.*" A tendency to pronounce both the /ŋ/ and /g/ sounds in the derived forms of *long, sing,* and *ring* is seen as correct, but the simple words *long, sing,* and *ring* do not end with this sound, *g* acting as a diacritic to indicate that *n* is pronounced /ŋ/.

/n/ may also be represented by *kn* and *gn* as in *knife, knot, know, gnaw, gnat,* and *gnome.* In these cases, *k* and *g* are silent, though the widespread publicity covering Evel Knievel's activities has caused many children to pronounce /k/ in such words as *knife* and *know*.

Such pronunciations suggest the influence of spelling on pronunciation, often developed unconsciously when decoding skill permits wide reading. Words are met, pronounced according to high-frequency grapheme-phoneme correspondences, made part of the spoken vocabulary, and are then often found to be incorrect according to common pronunciations.

The grapheme *gn* occurs not only in the initial and final position of words where its sound is always /n/ but also in medial positions between vowels where it usually represents /n/ and /g/. *Recognize, signal,* and *ignite* are a few of the words that appear in reading materials before grade five. Although *gn* in the final position of words such as *sign, malign,* and *resign* is pronounced /n/ and maintains this pronunciation in derivatives such as *signed, signing,* or *resigned,* it changes to reflect the /n/ and /g/ pronunciations in *signal* or *resignation,* which children may meet fairly early in reading materials. In these cases, the *g* is morpho-phonemic.

In contrast to *gn, kn* is always pronounced /n/ and occurs principally in initial positions, though it may occur as part of a compound in medial positions in such words as *penknife* and *bowknot.*

s

Although the letter *s* has two frequent pronunciations, /s/ and /z/, it also represents the sounds /sh/ and /ʒ/. Some fairly reliable rules help to distinguish between these usages, but, in most cases, there are no practical ways of distinguishing between them for beginning readers. Wijk (1966), for example, proposes a complex of rules that would only serve to raise unnecessary difficulties if used to teach the beginner.

In the initial position of words, *s* is used to represent the sound heard in the initial position of *Santa* except in the words *sure* and *sugar* and their derivatives (these rarely appear in children's materials). The teacher should rely on the child's ability to recognize familiar units when the derivatives *insure* or *sugary* occur.

In the final position, *s* may represent /s/ or /z/ with about equal regularity. The letter *s* in the final position of words is a morpheme, or inflectional ending, when it represents the meaning "more than one," in such words as *cats* and *books,* or "belongs to," in such words as *cat's* and *ship's.* The sound it represents varies: when it follows a voiceless sound, it is voiceless, that is, represents /s/; when it follows a voiced sound, it is usually voiced, that is, represents /z/. But *s* in the final position is not always a morpheme, as seen in such words as *is, as, was, this, yes, bus, us, circus,* and *famous.* The teacher can help children to distinguish when the letter *s* in a final position does or does not represent a morpheme, but children must be encouraged to be flexible in trying the sounds this symbol represents in decoding from print to sound.

The final silent *e* is identified as a diacritic in this generalization: the *e* at the end of words ending in *s* usually indicates that *s* is not a morpheme and that it can be pronounced either as the *s* in *Santa* or *z* in *zebra.* Try the /s/ *(Santa)* first. This generalization has 100 percent utility, but it requires the child to try alternative pronunciations. The rule can be abbreviated since the child would rarely have to identify the words in which *s* is not a morpheme. Thus:

GENERALIZATION: The *e* following *s* at the end of words indicates that *s* can be pronounced as /s/, *Santa,* or /z/, *zebra.* Try the /s/ sound first.

Despite the efforts of a few modern linguists to show that the final *e* was added by early lexicographers to indicate that the letter *s* never came at the end of words unless it was a morpheme, words in early use often ended in *s* while the *e*-ending of words was pronounced. The addition of *e* to *s*-ending words often was made by early lexicographers without historical justification. Because the number of words ending in *s* is now small, we can, however, rewrite the generalization to cover the above.

GENERALIZATION: The *e* following *s* at the end of words indicates that *s* almost never comes at the end of a word and can be pronounced as the /s/ in *Santa* or the /z/ in *zebra.* Try the /z/ sound first.

Note that the /z/ sound becomes predominant in this instructional version of the generalization.

The double *s* in medial or final position of such words as *kiss, miss, hiss, lesson, dress, class, grass,* and *kindness* is typically pronounced /s/ but also may be pronounced /z/, as seen in *dessert, passes,* and *scissors.* Again, there is no way to predict the pronunciation.

Although *s* in the initial position is pronounced as /ʃh/, as in *sure* and *sugar*, *s* in medial position of words alternates the /ʃh/ with the /ʒ/ sound, the /ʒ/ sound predominating. For example: *treasure, pleasure, measure, exposure, vision, television, usual,* and *casual* as opposed to *censure, erasure, mansion, sensual,* and *sensuous.* Except for the existence of words in which *s* is followed by *i,* it might be possible to say that *s* followed by *u* in medial positions of words is usually pronounced /ʃh/. It is, however, possible to account for both and say: "the letters *u* and *i* following *s* in medial positions of words act as diacritics to indicate that *s* may be pronounced either as /ʒ/ or /ʃh/; try the /ʒ/ sound first." This generalization also allows a pronunciation of *ssi* and *ssu* to be identified. Also see diacritic *i* and *u,* discussed in Chapter 5.

t

The letter *t* (or *tt*) usually represents the initial sound common to *ten, top,* and *table* except before *i* in unstressed syllables, where it frequently represents the /ʃh/ sound; before *e* and *u* in unstressed syllables, where it also represents the /ʃh/ sound; and before *h,* where it may represent the /th/ or /ŧh/ sounds. In these three cases, the letters *u, i,* and *h* may be said to be diacritics that signal these unusual pronunciations. *t* before *i* is described by Wijk (1966) as part of that group of spellings (*ci, ce, si, ssi,* etc.) that were originally pronounced as /s/ plus /y/ but that toward the end of the Middle English period changed to /ʃh/.

However, Pitman (1968:91) points out that when we

> examine those improvised spellings we notice that the scholarly writers and printers so often varied their improvisation, basing them upon the Latin spellings to which they were normally used. For instance, the improvisation for the sound /ʃh/ (which the Romans did not speak and for which the printers in England had no character) follows those Latin derivations which were common knowledge to the scribe and printer. The Bible begins with the *Creation of the World;* and *t* was used for /ʃh/ only because of the Latin word *creatus. Oceanus* is a Latin word, so *c* was also used for /ʃh/ in our *ocean,* also *ss* in *passion, sci* in *conscience.*

The implication is that these spellings exist for no other reason than false etymology, and, indeed, a variety of spellings can be traced to this lack of scholarship. While we can bemoan this lack of scholarship for foisting on us a welter of inadequate spellings, an investigation of *t* and *i* in unstressed syllables such as *tion, tial,* and *tience* indicates that *t* before *i* represents /ʃh/ whether it is found in *nation, education, definition, patience, patient, partial, superstitious, nasturtium, militia, initiate, ratio,* or *initiative.* Although it may seem desirable to simply teach that *ti* represents /ʃh/, the first *ti* in *superstitious* does not follow this pronunciation; and the *i* in *initiate* is pronounced, whereas in words like *partial* and *partiality,* it is alternatively silent or pronounced. In the latter case, the morphophonemic nature of *i* is apparent; it has the dual purpose of signaling that the *t* is to be pronounced /ʃh/ and of representing the /ɛɛ/, *eagle,* sound, as heard in unaccented syllables. For these reasons, the following generalization is more useful than any other in decoding from the print *ti* to the sound /ʃh/.

GENERALIZATION: The *i* following *t* in the last part of a word is usually silent and indicates that the *t* is pronounced /ʃh/.

This generalization has over 98 percent utility. The exceptions are *digestion, indigestion,* and *Christian,* where the signaled sound is /ch/, and *partiality,* previously discussed. This generalization covers all the usages in the Rinsland vocabulary, but it certainly does not preclude teaching that the pattern *tion* usually represents /ʃhun/, as often recommended to teachers. Yet, instruction on the multiple usages of the diacritic *i* is desirable.

Although *th* is commonly referred to in reading materials as a digraph, research on the use of *h* as a diacritic allows us to recognize the multiple uses of *h* and specifically its usage here to signal the change from the common pronunciations of *t* to /ᵺh/ or /þh/. The /ᵺh/ sound as in *feather* is the more frequent in discourse, owing to the multiple usages of the words *the, that,* and *this,* but it is least frequent when isolated words are studied. In the initial position, *th* is usually pronounced /þh/, *thumb,* except in *they, them, their, these, those, this, that, than, there, though, although, thus,* and *the.* This pronunciation of *th,* /þh/, is usually found at the end of words as well, except when followed by *e* and in a few exceptional cases. When the diacritic *e* follows *th,* the *e* signals that the voiced sound /ᵺh/ is to be pronounced (see diacritic *e,* p. 53), but the words *smooth* /smoᵒᵒᵺh/ and *mouth* (when used as a verb) /mouᵺh/ are exceptions to this finding. In the case of *with,* both pronunciations exist /withþ, wiᵺh/ with about equal regularity in American speech, but /wiᵺh/ is listed by most dictionaries as the more frequently used.

In the medial position, *th* may represent either /ᵺh/ or /þh/ with equal regularity in a group of words, though it is more likely to be /ᵮh/ in words of more frequent usage and of Anglo-Saxon origin; for instance, *father, mother, brother, other, feather, farther, gather, rather, weather, whether,* and *together.* Examples of words less commonly used and of foreign origin are: *athlete, author, method, sympathy, enthusiasm, anthology,* and *cathedral.*

x

As noted in Table 7, *x* has two frequent pronunciations: /ks/ as in *axe* and /gz/ as in *exact,* but it actually represents a total of six phonemes or phoneme pairs as shown below. It may also be silent, and in the word *x-ray* it represents /eks/.

x = /k/ in *excite* /eksiet/
x = /z/ in *xylophone* /zielufœn/
x = /ks/ in *box* /boks/
x = /gz/ in *exit* /egzit/, *exhaust* /egzaust/
x = /kʃh/ in *anxious* /aŋkʃhus/
x = /kʒ/ in *luxury* /lukʒureє/; also correct as /lukʃhureє/
x = /gʒ/ in *luxuriant* /lugʒœreєunt/
x = /sᴔ/ in *Sioux* (*x* is silent)

In general, the /ks/ pronunciation should be given when *x* comes at the end of a word or is followed by a consonant. If it were possible to teach children rules of stress prior to acquisition of skill in decoding, we might also note that the /ks/ sounds of *x* are usually found also where the principle stress falls on the vowel preceding *x.* A recognition of stress would also allow instruction that the /gz/ sounds of *x* occur when *x* is followed by a stressed vowel. Since stress or accent is a skill of doubtful use to native speakers of the language, and since exceptions do occur, simplification of instruction should be emphasized.

The teacher could note that the /gz/ sound of *x* is usually pronounced when *x* comes before *h* (*exhaust, exhibit*); that the /k/ sound of *x* is given when *x* comes before *c* (*excite, exceed, excellent, except, excuse*); that the /z/ sound of *x* is given when *x* begins a word and precedes a vowel (*xylophone, Xerox*); that the /kʃh/ sound is usually given when *x* is followed by *i* (*anxious*); that the /gʒ/ or /kʃh/ sounds are usually given when *x* is followed by *u* (*luxuriant, luxury*); and that at the end of words *x* represents /ks/ (*box*). In all other instances, *x* represents /ks/ or /gz/, and both should be tried until a word familiar to the child is decoded.

y

The letter *y* stands for the consonant sound /y/ only 3 percent of the time it is used, and then it appears chiefly at the beginning of words. In medial positions, it appears at the beginning of the second word of a two-word compound. *Yard, yes, yet, you,* and *year* are examples of words where the initial sound is /y/, and *dooryard* and *barnyard* are examples of the /y/ in a medial position. The usage of /y/ in *lawyer, canyon,* and *buoyant* indicates that *y* may also begin a syllable, but this occurs infrequently. Equally correct alternative pronunciations of *buoyant* /bɑiunt, bɔi-yunt/ permit the teacher to instruct children that the *y* begins syllables only in such words as *lawyer, sawyer,* and *canyon.*

As suggested in Table 7, however, *y* is largely used to represent the vowel sounds /ɛɛ/, /ie/, and occasionally /u/. Research has demonstrated that *y* is used to represent vowel sounds about 97 percent of the time. The vowel uses of *y* will be discussed in detail in Chapter 4.

z

The letter *z* is used most frequently to represent the sound /z/ *zebra* in a fairly large number of words in the initial, medial, or final position; however, the /z/ sound is far more frequently represented by the letter *s*. *z* represents /s/ in a few words, such as *chintz, quartz,* and *waltz*. *z* represents /ts/ in some other words, *Nazi* and *scherzo,* for instance. With a following diacritic *i* or *u, z* represents /ʒ/, as in *brazier, glazier,* and *seizure.* For purposes of initial reading instruction, however, the teacher should focus on encouraging association of /z/ with the letter *z* and refer to the infrequent pronunciations only as the words arise in print.

OTHER CONSONANT SOUNDS

Table 7, although complete in its consideration of the consonant letters of the alphabet, incompletely records the consonant sounds since the sounds /ʧ/, /ʃh/, /ŋ/, and /ʒ/ have no single-letter counterpart in the alphabet. /ʧ/, /ʃh/, and /ʒ/ have been dealt with as indicated below:

/ʧ/ represented by *t*; *t* plus diacritic *i*

/ʃh/ represented by *s*; *s* plus diacritic *i*; *t* plus diacritic *i*

/ʒ/ represented by *g*; *s* plus diacritic *i* and *u*; *z* plus diacritic *i* and *u*

/ʒ/ has been covered completely; and the *c* and *h* as /ʧ/ and the *s* and *h* as /ʃh/ have been covered adequately in the discussion of the character *h*; but some additional comments can be made on these, and /ŋ/ has been only partially dealt with.

ch

The combination *ch* in *chair*, *chic*, and *Christmas* represents the phonemes /ʧ/, /ʃh/, and /k/, as indicated earlier. There are no hard and fast rules for predicting the sounds that *ch* represents, except that before a consonant, the pronunciation is always /k/. All these phonemes are represented in initial, medial, or final positions, and /ʧ/ can be represented by *tch*, as in *match*, *watch*, and *itch*. Historically, the *t* is redundant in such words, but it would serve no useful purpose to call this to children's attention. Both *tch* and *ch* should be associated with /ʧ/, but the letter *t* can also be described as a diacritic to indicate that the following *ch* is pronounced /ʃh/.

sh

The digraph *sh* represents only the sound /ʃh/ in all positions of words. In words like *mishap*, the *sh* does not represent the digraph; instead, each symbol represents its own most frequent phoneme. Words such as these are few in number and rarely occur in children's material.

ŋ

The consonant phoneme /ŋ/ is a departure from the pattern used previously in that, heretofore, the consonant letters were identified as representing a variety of sounds. Recall the earlier discussion of *n* used to represent /ŋ/ before /k/ when represented either by *c*, *k*, *q*, or *x*. Note too that the grapheme *ng*, occurring only in the medial or final position of words, completes the listing of the graphemes used to represent this sound.

Although *ng* most often represents the /ŋ/ phoneme in the final position of words *(ring, sing, thing, hang, song, long, young,* and *lightning),* it is also used in the medial position frequently. These medial positions often cause children some pronunciation difficulties since it is not often realized that the *n* of *ng* in the words *English, finger, angle, linger, linguist,* or *language* represents /ŋ/ and that the *g* represents /g/. But *ng* represents /ŋ/ in *long* and /ŋg/ in *longer* and *longest,* as identified by a variety of dictionaries. *Finger* is written /fiŋ-gur/, *angle* as /aŋ-gul/, *language* as /laŋ-gwij/, and *longer* as /loŋ-gur/ (Barnhardt, 1950). The child who persists in saying the syllables *long* and *er* as /loŋ/ and /gur/ is quite correct, yet he or she is often corrected needlessly, and no correction of the incorrect syllables /fiŋ/ and /ur/ in *finger* is given. In fact, when the child realizes that *n* often represents the phoneme /ŋ/ no such "corrections" should be given, since only the expert can tell when /g/ should not be sounded as part of the second syllable.

The unusual spelling of *nd* for /ŋ/ in *handkerchief* is of interest because it is a single spelling for this sound. However, it would need little instructional consideration.

qu *and* que

In Table 7, *q* was identified as representing only the /k/ sound. The graphemes *qu* and *que* use *u* as a consonant. Most often, *qu* represents the phoneme pair /kw/ but also the phoneme /k/ where the *u* is silent. The /kw/ phoneme pair is found in *quiet, quick, quill, queen, queer, question, square, squeeze,* and so on, and the /k/ alone is found in *quay* /kεε/, *croquette, mosquito,* and *antique.*

The grapheme *que* is almost always found as the terminal spelling of words and in all cases represents /k/. Some authors hold that the *u* in these and in *gue* spellings represents a marker inserted by earlier lexicographers to indicate that the *e* is silent and that the *e* signals the glided, or "long," sound of the preceding vowel. In other words, there are two diacritic letters, *u* indicating that *e* is silent and *e* indicating that the preceding vowel is "long." All English *que* spellings are of French origin, imposed perhaps by the Norman French or adopted under their influence. A study of the effects of the final *e* on *que*-ending words in the Rinsland list indicates that *e* signals a glided or "long" vowel sound only 50 percent of the time, and that only in *antique* could we say *u* is morphophonemic.

i *and* u *As Consonants*

The use of *i* as a consonant, like the use of *y* as a vowel, has been little recognized by modern writers of instructional materials, and *u* as a consonant has been ignored. In a restudy of the Hanna et al. word corpus, Burmeister (1969) noted that the letter *i* represented the consonant phoneme /y/ 66 times out of 1,141 consonant occurrences, whereas my study of the Rinsland list showed a lower number, as might be expected, since the word corpus was smaller. Both studies, however, agree on the main findings that *i* represents the consonant phoneme /y/ in such words as *union, opinion, senior, brilliant, bullion, civilian, junior, onion, million, spaniel,* and *stallion,* whereas *e* represents the consonant /y/ only in the word *azalea*.

The letter *u* represents the consonant phoneme /w/ in *liquid, quiet, quick, queen, quill, suite, suave, language,* and *penguin* 243 times in the Hanna corpus. As part of the consonant cluster *qu, u* appears 27 times, where it is silent. It represents the consonant /w/ 5.5 percent of the time in the Rinsland corpus.

Thus, both *i* and *u* as consonants cannot be ignored in instruction and should be taught as both consonants and vowels.

i *and* u *As Diacritics*

The function of *i* following *c, s, ss, sc, t,* and *x* and the *u* after *s* and *ss* as diacritics is supported by additional research. In the Rinsland list, 423 words were identified as containing the graphemes *ci, si, ssi, sci, ti,* and *xi*. Occasionally, as in the words *appreciate* or *partiality,* the *i* served the dual purpose of indicating that the preceding consonant represented the phoneme /ʃh/ and that *i* also represented a vowel sound. Only five exceptions to this generalization were found—*digestion, indigestion, Christian, Christians,* and *juicier*—and in four of these the sound of *t* is seen as representing the /ʤh/ sound.

GENERALIZATION: The *i* following *c, s, ss, sc, t,* and *x* in the last part of a word is a diacritic indicating that these consonants represent the /ʃh/ sound.

This generalization was found to have almost 99 percent utility.

The letter *u*, tentatively identified as a diacritic after *s* and *ss*, is rejected in favor of the use of diacritic *e* to show the pronunciation of *s* + *ss* as /ʃh/ (see Chapter 4), yet the *u* as a diacritic is not rejected.

In the Rinsland corpus, *u* following *g* and *q* was found to be silent almost 2 percent of the time. In the case of *g* in such words as *guess, guide, guilty, fatigue, league*, or *tongue, u* appeared to act as a diacritic to indicate that the *g* was pronounced /g/ rather than /j/. Since, as was pointed out earlier, *g* before *e, i*, and *y* usually represents /j/, whereas *g* before *u, o*, and *a* is pronounced /g/, the *u* as a diacritic after *g* and before *e* or *i* signals the /g/ while remaining silent itself. In *gue*-ending words, *u* is used to cancel out the effect of the final *e* since *e* after *g* at the end of words serves as a diacritic to indicate that the *g* is pronounced /j/ or that the *ng*, normally used to represent /ŋ/, represents /nj/. (See also diacritic *e*, Chapter 4.)

THE SILENT CONSONANTS

It has been said that every letter of the alphabet is silent at some time or another. A variety of the consonants have already been singled out as silent in the preceding discussion, but it is helpful to bring them together for easier reference. Often, consonants are silent because pronunciation has changed over the years, whereas spelling has been held fairly stable by the dictionaries. Silent consonants may also occur because English has borrowed heavily from foreign sources, retaining the spellings of words but modifying their pronunciations, or because scholars of earlier periods inserted consonants based on false etymology. Changes in spelling have taken place slowly, but as yet there has been no wholesale elimination of silent consonants. For example, *ue* has been dropped from *catalog* and *epilog, f* has been substituted for *gh* in *draft*, as in *draft beer* (as opposed to the antique *draught*), and *c* has been substituted for *qu* in *licorice*.

b. The *b* is generally silent before *t* and after *m* in such words as *debt, doubt, subtle, lamb, climb, comb, crumb, dumb*, and *thumb*. It was originally inserted before *t* based on false etymology, and the usage has remained. Some linguists argue that the *b* after *m* is morpho-phonemic and serves a useful purpose since, etymologically, the root *bomb* can be identified, as in *bombard* and *bombardier*. Unfortunately, this argument does not hold for *comb-*

ing, combed, plumbing, plumber, climbing, climbed, tomb, numb, thumb, and *dumb,* among others. And, of course, to identify the root *bomb* in *bombaceous* or *bombazine* would be terribly misleading as to the meaning of the words. The *b* after *m* is pronounced, however, in other words, such as *rhombus, amber, lumber, number, timber, nimble, tumble,* and *mumble.* In general, the *b* is silent before *t* and after *m* at the end of words but not when *mb* occurs in the medial position of words.

c. The *c* is silent only occasionally, as in *indict,* whether pronounced /indie/ or /indiet/, in one spelling of /vi-tulz/ *victuals,* in the second *c* of *Connecticut,* and in the grapheme *ck* in *sick, trick,* and so on.

ch. As noted earlier, *ch* is silent in *yacht.*

d. The *d* is always silent in *handkerchief, handsome,* and *Wednesday;* often also in *grandfather* and *grandmother,* where it is sloughed off as superfluous in some pronunciations.

g. As seen earlier, *g* is silent in the digraph *gn* but it is also silent in *gm* at the end of such words as *diaphragm* and *phlegm.* The *g* is pronounced, however, in *engine, diaphragmatic,* or *phlegmatic.*

h. The *h* is usually silent in *heir, honest, horror,* and *hour* and their derivatives, but it is not uncommon to hear some American speakers pronounce the *h* in the first three words. They are apparently influenced by the spelling. It is always silent in the digraph *rh* and *kh* and usually silent following *x* in such words as *exhaust* or *exhibit.* It is also frequently silent between a consonant and the unglided, "short," or unstressed vowel, as in *shepherd* or *forehead,* and after vowels at the end of such words as *ah, bah,* and *hurrah.*

k. The *k* is usually silent before *n* in the initial position of words and in the root word *know* of *acknowledge.* The *ck* is lost in the pronunciation of *blackguard* /blagard/. Note, however, that the *k* is pronounced in *Knesset,* the Israeli parliament.

l. The letter *l* is generally silent before *f, k, m,* and *v,* as seen in *half, talk, calm, halves,* and *salve.* It is also silent in *would, should,* and *could* but is considered part of the spelling for /d/ in these words by some authors. It might better be considered part of the spelling of *ou* in these words since so many authors suggest that *l* influences the sound of the preceding vowel. In this sense, *l* might be considered a diacritic letter that is silent.

m. The letter *m* appears to be silent only in the word *mnemonic.*

n. The *n* is silent after *m* in *autumn, column, condemn, damn,* and *hymn,* among others, but it is considered morpho-phonemic since it signals its own pronunciation in the derivations *autumnal, columnar, condemnation, damnation,* and *hymnal.*

p. The *p* is silent before *n, s,* and *t* in a variety of words, for example, *pneumonia, psalm, ptomaine, psychology,* and *pseudo-.*

s. The *s* is generally silent after *i* in such words as *aisle, isle, island, chamois, debris,* and *chassis.* It is also silent in the final position in *Arkansas.*

t. The *t* is always silent in words containing *stle* or *sten* endings, as illustrated by such words as *fasten, glisten, christen, listen, castle, whistle,* and *rustle.* It can be pronounced or not pronounced in *often,* /ofen, often/, and *soften;* either alternative is correct, though the first occurs more frequently than the second. The *t* is also silent in words chiefly of French origin that end with *et, ot,* or *ut,* for example, *bouquet, croquet, ballet, depot, debut, mortgage,* and *esprit,* as in *esprit de corps.*

th. The digraph *th* is occasionally silent, as in *asthma* and *isthmus.*

u. The *u* is often silent after *g* and *q,* acting as a diacritic in the former case and as part of the French spelling of /k/ in *que* endings. The *u* is also silent after *g* in *guard, guarantee,* and *guardian,* in which it serves no diacritic function.

w. While *w* is often identified as acting as a vowel in such combinations as *ow, ew,* and *aw* (see Chapter 4), its consonant usage is found only before vowels and before the consonant *r.* The *w* before *r,* found only in the initial position of words, was at one time pronounced but now is silent. It is found in such words as *write, wrist, wring,* and *wrong.*

The *w* is also silent when it falls between a consonant and a vowel as seen in such words as *answer, sword,* and *two.* It may also be regarded as silent in the pattern *wh,* where it represents the phoneme /h/ in such words as *who, whom, whose,* and *whole.*

x and *z.* The *x* is silent in *Sioux;* the *z* is silent in *rendezvous.*

REFERENCES

Anderson, Irving H., and Dearborn, Walter F. *The Psychology of Reading.* New York: Ronald Press, 1952. Chapter 5.

Bailey, Mildred H. "The Utility of Phonic Generalizations in Grades One Through Six." *The Reading Teacher* 20 (1967): 413–418.

Barnhardt, Clarence L. *The American College Dictionary.* New York: Harper and Brothers, 1950.

Bridge, J. T. "Rank-ordering of Letters and Letter Combinations According to Ease of Learning Their Sound Associations." Master's thesis, University of Texas, 1968.

Burmeister, Lou E. "Usefulness of Phonic Generalizations." *The Reading Teacher* 21 (1968): 349 – 356, 360.

———. "The Effect of Syllabic Position on the Phonemic Behavior of Single Vowel Graphemes." *Reading and Realism,* IRA Proceedings, Vol. 13, Part I, 1969, 645 – 649.

Clymer, Theodore. "The Utility of Phonic Generalizations in the Primary Grades." *The Reading Teacher* 16 (1963): 252 – 258.

Clymer, Theodore, and Barrett, Thomas C. *My Sound and Word Book,* Reading 360 Series. Boston: Ginn, 1969.

Coleman, Edmund. "Data Base for a Reading Technology." Monograph, *Journal of Educational Psychology,* 1972.

Dewey, Godfrey. *Relative Frequency of English Speech Sounds.* Cambridge, Mass.: Harvard University Press, 1923.

———. *Relative Frequency of English Spellings.* New York: Columbia University, Teachers College Press, 1970.

Dewey, Godfrey, Mazurkiewicz, Albert J., and Tanyzer, H. *mie alfabet buk.* New York: i/t/a Publications, 1963.

Emans, Robert. "The Usefulness of Phonic Generalizations Above the Primary Grades." *The Reading Teacher* 20 (1967): 419 – 425.

Gates, Arthur I. *The Improvement of Reading.* New York: Macmillan, 1947.

Gibson, Eleanor J. "Learning to Read." In *Theoretical Models and Processes in Reading,* edited by Harry Singer and Robert Ruddel. Newark, Del.: International Reading Association, 1970.

Gove, Philip, ed. Webster's *Third New International Dictionary.* Springfield, Mass.: G. & C. Merriam Co., 1966.

Hanna, Paul R., et al. *Phoneme-Grapheme Correspondences as Cues to Spelling Improvement.* Washington, D.C.: U.S. Office of Education, Bureau of Research, 1966.

Harris, Albert J., and Jacobson, Milton D. *Basic Elementary Reading Vocabularies.* New York: Macmillan, 1972.

Heilman, Arthur W. *Phonics in Proper Perspective.* Columbus, Ohio: Merrill, 1968.

Mazurkiewicz, Albert J. "The Diacritic *e.*" *Reading World* 14 (October 1974): 9 – 21.

———. "Applicability of Diacritic *e* Generalizations." *Reading World* 14 (December 1974): 104 – 111.

Mazurkiewicz, A. J., and Tanyzer, H. *The Early to Read – i.t.a. Series.* New York: i/t/a/ Publications, 1963, 1964.

Pitman, Sir James. "The Initial Teaching Alphabet in Historical Perspective." *New Perspectives in Reading Instruction,* edited by Albert J. Mazurkiewicz. New York: Pitman, 1968.

Rinsland, Henry D. *A Basic Vocabulary of Elementary School Children.* New York: Macmillan, 1945.

Wijk, Axel. *Rules of Pronunciation for the English Language.* London: Oxford University Press, 1966.

4
The Vowels

Earlier, it was pointed out that the consonant phonemes in American English are represented by fewer graphemes than are the vowel phonemes. The count of 168 consonant graphemes in Table 3 can be contrasted with the 265 vowel graphemes identified in Table 9. Consonant sounds in words are pronounced with regularity from region to region in the United States, but vowel phonemes in a given word can vary markedly. For example, the word *been* is pronounced /bin, ben, bɛɛn/; *suit* can be /syɷt, sɷt/. Such differences will be discussed at later points in this chapter, but for now it is important simply to recognize them. Only one pronunciation of a grapheme in a word is listed, avoiding artificially inflating the number of graphemes that might be said to exist to represent the vowel phonemes.

The vowel phoneme was defined as a speech-sound made without obstructing the flow of air and fifteen (or sixteen, when /a/ *arm* is treated as different from /o/ *not*) significant vowel phonemes were identified in General American Speech. The problems of instruction on vowel grapheme-phoneme correspondence for decoding is compounded by the fact that any one phoneme may be represented

TABLE 9. Vowel Phonemes and Their Most Frequent Spellings #

Phoneme	Graphemes	Examples
/a/	a, a-e, aa, ah, ai, au, a-ue, i, i-ue, ua	had, have, baa, dahlia, plaid, laugh, harangue, lingerie, meringue, guarantee
/ɑ/	a, aa, a-e, ah, au, e, ea, i, ua	part, bazaar, are, ah, taunt, sergeant, heart, memoir, guard
/æ/	a, a-e, ai, ai-e, aigh, a-u, a-ue, au, au-e, ay, e, é, e-e, ea, ee, eh, ei, ei-e, eigh, er, et, ey, hei, ie, ue, uet	making, made, main, raise, straight, plaguing, plague, gauging, gauge, may, re, attaché, there, great, matinee, eh, their, Seine, weigh, dossier, ballet, they, heir, lingerie, applique, bouquet
/au/	a, a-e, ah, ao, au, au-e, augh, aw, awe, hau, o, o-e, o-ue, oa, ough	fall, false, hurrah, extraordinary, haul, because, taught, saw, awe, exhaust, for, gone, tongue, broad, thought
/e/	a, ae, ai, ay, e, e-e, ea, ea-e, ei, eo, ie, u, ue	many, diaeresis, said, says, men, ledge, head, cleave, heifer, leopard, friend, bury, guess
/ɛɛ/	ae, e, e-e, ea, ea-e, ea-ue, ee, ee-e, ei, ei-e, eo, ey, i, i-e, i-ue, ie, ie-e, is, it, oe, uay, ui, y, agh, ois	aeon, be, these, each, leave, league, see, cheese, receipt, receive, people, key, si, marine, antique, grief, believe, debris, esprit, amoeba, quay, mosquito, funny, shillelagh, chamois
/i/	a, a-e, ai, e, e-e, ee, ehe, ei, hi, i, i-e, ia, ia-e, ie-e, o, u, u-e, ui, y-e	imaging, image, mountain, pretty, college, been, forehead, forfeit, exhibit, in, give, marriages, marriage, sieve, women, busy, minute, built, apocalypse
/ie/	ai-e, ay, aye, ei, eigh, ey, eye, i, i-e, ia, ie, igh, oy, ui, ui-e, uy, y, y-e, ye	aisle, kayak, aye, stein, height, geyser, eye, kind, time, diamond, lie, high, coyote, guiding, guide, buy, by, type, dye
/o/	a, au, eau, ho, o, o-e, o-ue, oh, ow	was, laurel, bureaucracy, honor, not, gone, dialogue, demijohn, knowledge
/œ/	au, au-e, eau, eo, ew, io, o, o-e, o-ue, oa, oa-e, oe, oh, oo, os, ot, ou, ou-e,	chauffeur, mauve, beau, yeoman, sew, mustachio, no, more, rogue, coal, coarse, toe, oh, floor, apropos, depot, four, course,

TABLE 9. Vowel Phonemes and Their Most Frequent Spellings # (Continued)

	ough, ow, owa, owe	th*ough*, kn*ow*, t*owa*rd, *owe*
/u/	o, o-e, ½o-e,* o-ue,	*o*ther, s*ome*, *one*, t*o*ng*ue*, d*oe*s,
	oe, oo, ou, u, u-e,	fl*oo*d, c*ou*ntry, b*u*t, j*u*dge,
	u-ue,	br*u*sq*ue*
	a, a-e, ai, au, e,	*a*bout, nuis*a*nce, mount*ai*n, rest*au*rant,
	e-e, ea, ea-e, ei,	*o*ver, lic*e*nse, *ea*rly, h*ea*rse,
	eo, eu, ha, he, i,	mull*ei*n, lunch*eo*n, connoiss*eu*r,
	i-e, ia, ie, io,	ging*ha*m, *he*rb, elix*i*r, eng*i*ne,
	½le, ½m, o-o, oa, oi,	parl*ia*ment, misch*ie*vous, fash*io*n,
	oi-e, ou-e, ua,	peop*le*, critic*i*sm, col*o*nel, cupb*oa*rd,
	ue, ueu, uo, y	connoiss*oi*er, porp*oi*se, sc*ou*rge, piq*ua*nt,
		lacq*ue*r, liq*ueu*r, liq*uo*r, mart*y*r
/ue/	eau, eu, eu-e, ew,	b*eau*tiful, f*eu*d, d*eu*ce, f*ew*, *ewe*,
	ewe, iew, u, u-e,	v*iew*, h*u*man, *u*se, f*ugue*, d*ue*,
	u-ue, ue, ueue, ui, ut	q*ueue*, s*ui*t, deb*ut*
/ω/	eu, o, oo, ou, oui,	pl*eu*risy, w*o*man, g*oo*d, sh*ou*ld,
	u, u-e	b*oui*llon, f*u*ll, s*u*re
/ꞷ/	eu, ew, ieu, o, o-e,	rh*eu*m, cr*ew*, l*ieu*, d*o*, m*o*ve,
	oe, oo, oo-e, ooh,	sh*oe*, t*oo*, l*oo*se, p*ooh*, s*ou*p,
	ou, ou-e, ough, oup,	r*ou*te, thr*ough*, c*ou*p, rendezv*ou*s,
	ous, u, eu, ue, ui,	tr*u*ly, man*eu*ver, tr*ue*, fr*ui*t, br*ui*se,
	ui-e, uo	b*uo*y
/oi/	oi, oi-e, oy, oy-e,	p*oi*nt, n*oi*se, b*oy*s, garg*oy*le,
	uoi-e, uoy	turq*uoi*se, haut*buoy*
/ou/	hou, ou, ou-e, ough,	*hou*r, *ou*t, h*ou*se, b*ough*, n*ow*
	ow	

*The use of ½ preceding the grapheme in this table indicates that the grapheme represents two sounds. Thus, ½*o-e* in *one* indicates that *o-e* represents both /w/ and /u/.

by from five to thirty-nine graphemes, with an average of sixteen graphemes per phoneme. Fortunately, many of the graphemes are used infrequently in children's materials and can be eliminated from consideration. Also, generalizations can be written to group a number of spelling patterns or to point out the functions of the vowel graphemes and thus simplify the task of decoding.

The vowel letters, typically identified as *a, e, i, o, u*, are more correctly identified as *a, e, i, o, y*, and often *u* and *w*. You will recall that *y* was identified as representing a vowel over 97 percent of the time and that *e, i*, and *o* had some consonantal usage (up to 11 percent in the case of *i*); and that *h* and *w* (as well as *y*) were considered semivowels. In combination with another vowel, *w*, for example, is said to represent a vowel sound.

The letter *h* was identified in Chapter 3 as a consonant and a diacritic; thus, it is no longer necessary to say that it is "sometimes a vowel letter." The letter *i* was also identified as a diacritic indicating pronunciations of consonants, but its main use is as a vowel letter. The letter *y*, used mostly to represent vowel sounds ranging from /u/ *(myrtle)* to /i/ *(myth)*, /ɛɛ/ *(funny)*, and /ie/ *(shy)*, has a limited consonant usage. It is also found in the second half of such vowel digraphs as *ay*, *ey*, *uy*, and *oy*, where it acts as part of the grapheme to represent the diphthongs /æ/, /ɛɛ/, /ie/, and /œ/. Its function here may be thought of as that of a diacritic, but there is no consistency in its usage to signal a particular phoneme. Note that *ay* represents /e/, /ie/, and /æ/ and that *ey* represents /ɛɛ/, /æ/, /ie/. The letter *y* when used as part of a vowel digraph may also be described as representing the ending glide of the diphthongs /ie/, /ōi/, /ɛɛ/, and /æ/ and the beginning glide of /ue/.

The letter *u* represents either /u/, *sun*, or /ue/, *mule*, a little less than 56 percent of the time in a study of its usages in the Rinsland *Basic Vocabulary* (1945). It acts as the consonant /w/ in *queen* more than 5 percent of the time, as a diacritic after *g* 2 percent of the time, and by itself or in combination with other vowel letters the remainder of the time to represent a variety of vowel phonemes. Its function here may be thought of as similar to those of the diacritic *y* and the semivowels *w* and *y* used as glides. The listing of the vowel letters in Webster's *Third New International Dictionary* excludes *u*, counting only *a*, *e*, *i*, and *o* as the four vowel letters. Short of a complete count of the usage of *u* in the over 500,000 words in that dictionary, the above evidence can be used as highly supportive of Editor Gove's position.

THE SIGNIFICANT VOWEL GRAPHEMES

Table 10 shows the frequency of grapheme occurrences for the vowel phonemes. It has been organized to include only those graphemes for each vowel phoneme which together, if learned, allow decoding of print with an average of over 97 percent accuracy. In her studies, Burmeister (1968a) suggests only an 80 to 90 per-

TABLE 10. Vowel Grapheme-Phoneme Occurrences in 100,000 Running Words

Phoneme	Number of Occurrences in Words	Total of Occurrences Accounted for by Graphemes	Graphemes and Their Percentage of Occurrence
/a/	1,565	99.5%	a (98.17), a-e (1.4)
/æ/	1,446	96.9	a (44.95), a-e (24.6), ai (17.6), ay (6.2), ea (1.7), eigh (1.3), ey (.8), aigh (.03)
/ɑ/	322	97.1	a (87.0), a-e (6.8), ea (3.3)
/au/	442	96.1	o (51.8), a (24.2), au (8.6), aw (7.7), augh (1.8)
/e/	3,172	98.8	e (92.7), ea (3.31), e-e (3.0)
/ɛɛ/	2,502	98.3	e (40.5), y (29.2), ea (11.7), ee (7.0), ie (6.8), e-e (1.8), ey (.9), i-e (.6), ei (.6)
/i/	4,281	98.6	i (88.9), y (3.6), i-e (3.5), a-e (2.2), w (.4)
/ie/	859	97.0	i (35.2), i-e (37.7), igh (8.6), y (8.5), ie (5.7), y-e (1.3)
/o/	1,103	97.8	o (92.7), a (3.2), o-e (1.9)
/œ/	1,188	96.6	o (63.4), o-o (15.4), ow (8.9), oa (6.0), ou (1.8), oe (1.1)
/u/	4,391	97.8	a (25.2), e (23.9), u (20.6), o (21.5), ou (3.8), i (1.3), a-e (1.8), ea (.7)
/ue/	469	95.5	u (68.5), u-e (21.5), ew (3.2), ue (2.3)
/ɔi/	105	100.0	oi (69.5), oy (30.5)
/ɔu/	256	96.1	ou (74.2), ow (21.9)

TABLE 10. Vowel Grapheme-Phoneme Occurrences in 100,000 Running Words (Continued)

Phoneme	Number of Occurrences in Words	Total of Occurrences Accounted for by Graphemes	Graphemes and Their Percentage of Occurrence
/ω/	368	99.7	u (54.3), oo (31.0), ou (6.8), o (4.6), u-e (3.0)
/ω̄/	453	94.4	oo (40.8), u (20.5), o (8.2), ou (6.4), u-e (7.5), ew (4.9), ue (3.5), ough (2.0), o-e (2.6)

SOURCE: Based on data from Dewey, *Relative Frequency of English Spellings.* New York: Columbia University, Teachers College Press, 1970. Supplemented with data from Hanna et al., *Phoneme-Grapheme Correspondences as Cues to Spelling Improvement.* Washington, D.C.: U.S. Office of Education, Bureau of Research, 1966.

cent utility to be desirable. As can be seen, however, the figure of 80 to 90 percent utility, when applied to the phoneme /æ/, for example, would exclude the graphemes *ea,* as in *great, eigh,* as in *weigh, ey,* as in *they,* and *aigh,* as in *straight,* from instructional consideration as among those least used. Yet, as will be seen in an examination of typical reading materials, such graphemes appear early and must be taught either as grapheme-phoneme correspondences or as "sight words." Only those graphemes that represented any one phoneme less than ten times were excluded. This procedure produces accuracies in decoding print to sound ranging from 94.4 to 100 percent. A total of 84 graphemes are used to present the 16 phonemes, with an average of 5.25 graphemes per phoneme. Six phonemes, /a/, /e/, /o/, /a/, /oi/, and /ou/, can be decoded using only 2 or 3 graphemes, whereas others require as many as 9.

Table 11 reorganizes the grapheme-phoneme information to show that only 35 *different* graphemes are used 97.4 percent of the time to represent the 16 phonemes of American English, a ratio of 35/16, or 2.2 graphemes for each phoneme. The problem of decoding print to sound may seem relatively easy when viewed in this way, but as inspection of Table 11 shows, one grapheme may represent as many as six different vowel phonemes.

Burmeister's (1968a) work is based on the frequency of occurrence in the Hanna et al. (1966) corpus of 17,310 words. When adjusted to the 16-phoneme base, her work is of value in understanding that, when lists of words are used in isolation for decoding instruction, certain graphemes have higher utilities than others, and

TABLE 11. Phonemes Represented by the Thirty-five Vowel Graphemes

Graphemes	Phonemes Represented
1. *a*	/a/, /æ/, /o/, /a/, /u/, /au/
2. a-e	/a/, /æ/, /i/, /ɑ/, /u/, /au/
3. oi	/æ/
4. ay	/æ/
5. ea	/æ/, /e/, /ɛ/, /a/, /u/
6. eigh	/æ/
7. ey	/æ/
8. aigh	/æ/
9. e	/e/, /ɛ/, /i/, /u/
10. e-e	/e/, /ɛ/
11. e	/ɛ/
12. ue	/ɛ/, /i/, /ie/
13. i-e	/ɛ/, /i/, /ie/
14. ei	/ɛ/
15. i	/i/, /ie/, /u/
16. y	/i/, /ɛ/, /ie/
17. igh	/ie/
18. y-e	/ie/
19. o	/o/, /u/, /ω/, /ω/, /au/
20. o-e	/o/, /œ/, /u/, /ω/
21. ow	/œ/, /ou/
22. oa	/œ/
23. ou	/œ/, /u/, /ou/, /ω/, /ω/
24. oe	/œ/
25. u	/u/, /ue/, /w/, /ω/
26. u-e	/ue/, /ω/, /ω/
27. ew	/ue/, /ω/
28. ue	/ue/
29. oi	/ɔi/
30. oy	/ɔi/
31. oo	/ω/, /ω/
32. au	/au/
33. aw	/au/
34. ough	/au/
35. augh	/au/

that the two-vowel generalization, "when two vowels go walking, the first does the talking," has limited usefulness. When such words are found in discourse or narrative material, the utility of a given grapheme changes markedly. Table 12, based on selected data Burmeister produced in a reversal of the Hanna et al. procedures,

TABLE 12. Percentage of Phoneme Occurrences for Selected Vowel-Pair Graphemes

Grapheme	Number of Occurrences in Word Corpus	Example	Phoneme	Number of Occurrences Representing Phoneme	Percentage of Occurrences Representing Phoneme
ei	86	reign	/æ/	24	40.0%
ey	69	they		15	21.7
ea	545	great		27	5.0
ea	545	feast, dear	/ɛɛ/	324	59.5
ei	86	receipt		22	25.6
ey	69	money, bey		48	66.7

shows that 3 graphemes are used to represent either of 2 common vowel phonemes, /æ/ and /ɛɛ/; that the grapheme *ei* is likely to represent /æ/ more often than /ɛɛ/; and that *ey* represents /æ/ almost one-fourth of the time the pattern was used. The pattern *ea*, representing /ɛɛ/, /e/, /u/, /æ/, /ɑ/, most often represents /ɛɛ/ but can be confused with /æ/ 5 percent of the time. Reform in the orthography is desirable, but procedures based on the usefulness of the 35 graphemes for the 16 vowel phonemes are available to simplify the child's burden.

NAMING AND CLASSIFYING VOWEL PHONEMES

The typical procedure, as seen earlier, has been to refer to vowels as long, short, and diphthongal, but, as seen as well, linguists criticize this procedure as misleading since vowels called "long" are diphthongal, and length refers to the duration of a vowel sound whether it is of the "long" or "short" variety. The sound /ɑ/, *arm*, is neither long nor short according to this classification system and has been called the broad *a*. The phoneme /ɑ/ might be considered an allophone of /o/, *dog*, since linguists often do not recognize it as a separate phoneme and often equate it with /o/. Other writers relate it to /aʊ/ and again do not recognize it as a separate phoneme. For this reason, it might also be called an allophone of /aʊ/. While I will consider all these phonemes as distinct in their own right for purposes of instruction, in my idiolect the sounds /ɑ/ and /o/ are the same. The reader should determine for himself or herself if the phonemes are distinctly different, similar to /o/ or /au/, or closely alike.

Table 13 shows the common designations of the vowel phonemes and should help the teacher to explain these different terms to children who may be confused. Because no set of standardized terms are agreed upon, confusion may result from meeting different authors' preferences or personal language constructs. For example, since the sound /æ/, *angel*, can be identified using all these terms, the simplest procedure, use of a key word to illustrate the sound and calling all vowel phonemes as vowels, might ordinarily be the easiest, with classification left to the lexicographers, phoneticians, or linguists. Reading instruction doesn't demand them except for ease in referring to a certain set when using generalizations. For my purpose the simplest procedure will be used whenever possible and later, I will utilize the terms *glided* or *long*, *unglided* or *short*.

Groff (1972), in describing syllables, indicates that "linguists seem to accept the notion of 'closed' or checked-vowel, and 'open' or free-vowel, syllables," and Venezky (1967) refers to free and checked vowels. Free and checked syllables may be useful to linguists who prefer not to use the *open* or *closed* terminology common among teachers, but the terms *free* and *checked* imply that there are no free vowel sounds in checked syllables. Such usage

TABLE 13.   Classifications of the Vowel Phonemes

Phoneme	Typical	Ruddell (1974)	Venezky (1967)	Soffietti (1968)	i.t.a.
/a/, /e/, /i/, /o/, /u/	short	unglided	checked	vowels	vowels
/ɑ/	broad (distinct)	unglided (related to /au/)	checked (related to /o/)	vowel (related to /o/)	vowel (distinct)
/æ/, /ɛɛ/, /œ/*	long	glided	free	vowel	vowel
/ie/, /ue/, /ou/, /oi/	diphthong	glided	free	phonemic cluster	vowel
/ω/	long	glided	free	vowel	vowel
/au/†	short	unglided	checked	vowel	vowel

*æ, ɛɛ, œ are also considered diphthongs by definition; see Chapter 1.

†/au/ is also referred to as a diphthong by some authors; see Burmeister (1968: 450).

for children can serve only to confuse since these terms describe vowel sounds as imprecisely as do the terms *long* or *short* and have no relevance to either acoustic or articulatory phenomena.

The term *glided* does accurately describe the articulatory procedures used to produce the vowel phonemes /æ/, /ie/, /œ/, and so on. Its companion, *unglided,* can be used to refer to those vowel phonemes that are produced without a gliding movement of the lips, tongue, and so forth. Since the usage, whether accurate or not, of the terms *long* and *short* has been so common in instruction for so many, their continued use as synonymous with *glided* and *unglided* can certainly be followed. However, there is no need to extend or continue the use of the word *diphthong,* since either *glided* or *long* (when thought of as synonymous) covers all references to vowel phonemes.

The Diacritic e

The phoneme represented by the *a* in *lady* and that by the *ai* in *air* are considered to be different phonemes by phoneticians, as are the *e* in *me* and *ea* in *hear.* These differences are sometimes shown in dictionaries as *ā, â, ē, ê* or even *ā, å, ē, ė,* where the vowel quality is described as half a long *a* or *e* or even as the long *a* or *e* before *r.* Some writers will therefore extend the listing of graphemes to include *ear, ere, eir,* and so on. As suggested by Table 10, linguists do not consider the /æ/ in *day* and *there* as significantly different since they are not listed. Since the /æ/ before *r* in *there* or *where* is identified as a mid-front vowel that includes the "long a" in its range of pronunciations, and since "long a" is also described as a mid-front vowel, it can be seen that the first is either identical to the second or an allophone of it. I will, accordingly, treat the /æ/ before *r* and so on as allophones of the basic phoneme and not distinguish between them. Such allophones are not encoded in any of the reformed orthographies, and extensive research has demonstrated no reason to distinguish them separately in relation to teaching the child to read. The demand for finer distinctions may be valid for adults, but it has no merit in relation to the child.

Secondary Generalizations as Applied to Vowels

The diacritic *e* has been shown to have a variety of graphic or relational meanings in respect to consonants. Its usage is also more frequent with consonants than with vowels (at least 52 percent of the time). It will be seen, however, that the diacritic *e* applies to ten of the thirty-five vowel graphemes. The classification of *e*-ending words can be summarized as follows:

1. Those words in which the diacritic *e* indicates a letter is never word-final.
2. Those words in which the diacritic *e* indicates a pronunciation of the adjacent consonant.
3. Those words in which the diacritic *e* indicates a pronunciation of a consonant once-removed.
4. Those words in which the diacritic *e* indicates a pronunciation of the adjacent vowel.
5. Those words in which the diacritic *e* indicates a pronunciation of the vowel once-removed.

The usage of glided or long and unglided or short in referring to the vowels can be extended to include /ɑu/ and /ɔi/ as glided or long vowels since "long" is seen to be synonymous with glided or diphthong and does not refer to length. It is important to understand this usage of "long" since we often think only of the vowels /æ/, /ɛɛ/, /ie/, /œ/, and /ue/ when the term is used, forgetting that /ω/, written as *oo* in *food*, is long and /ω/, written as *oo* in *good*, is short. The usage is important when referring to such words as *toe*, *shoe*, or *blue*, in applying the diacritic *e*. In the case of *toe*, the *e* indicates that the vowel letter represents the glided or long *o* /œ/; in *shoe*, the letter *o* represents the glided or long vowel /ω/; in *blue*, the *u* represents the glided or long vowel /ω/.

GENERALIZATION: The *e* following a vowel at the end of words indicates that the first vowel has a glided or long sound.

The application of this rule to such words as *tie, lie, die, toe, floe, see, bee, flee, tree, flue, blue,* and *true* is instantly recognizable, and the rule has almost 87 percent utility. The exceptions, such as *matinee, antique, unique, mosque, catalogue, dialogue, fatigue, plague,* and *league,* fall into three categories:

1. French loan words *(matinee)*, where *e* is pronounced /æ/.
2. French loan words *(antique)*, where *que* represents /k/.
3. Words ending in *gue*, where the *u* is a diacritic used only to separate the *e* from the *g*.

If we were to exclude *gue* and *que* words, the generalization is seen to have almost 100 percent utility. We must, however, remember that the letters *o* and *u* must be taught as representing /ɷ/ and /ue/ and /ɷ/, respectively, since the vowel letters do multiple duty.

GENERALIZATION: The *e* following a vowel and a consonant (vce, vowel-consonant-plus *e*, patterns) other than the consonants *c, g, l, ng, s, th, v,* and *z* and the pattern *ur* indicates that the preceding vowel has a glided or long sound.

There are some guidelines to help determine the vowel sounds in the exceptions to this generalization. However, the rule itself has wide applicability, with a utility covering almost 84 percent of the words where vce patterns exist. Most of the exceptions, not discussed previously, are as follows: *delicate, accurate, chocolate, climate, definite, exquisite, favorite, granite;* and *one, anyone, someone, wholesome, everyone, troublesome, come, become, done, none, overcome, handsome, begone.*

The major exceptions fall into two categories:

1. Those words in which the last syllable is unstressed, consonant plus *ate* or *ite*, and in which, therefore, the vowel sound is short *i.*
2. Those words in which the vowel letter *o* is pronounced /wu/ or /u/ and includes the words *one, come,* or *some.*

Other exceptions previously discussed involve *gue-* and *que-*ending words, French loan words such as *mature,* and miscellaneous words such as *massacre, mustache, crèche,* or *fete.*

In the first group, the *e* has a graphical function, but it is also morpho-phonemic in some words and indicates the alternative pronunciation of such word pairs as:

/i/	/æ/
certificate	certificate
predicate	predicate
associate	associate
scholastic	scholastic
alternate	alternate

In the second group, the *e* has only a graphical usage, though at one time it was inflected. When the words *one, some,* and *come* are

learned as sight words, all the compound words are easily pronounced, despite the presence of the final *e*.

VOWEL GRAPHEME-PHONEME CORRESPONDENCES

The vowel letters of the alphabet—*a, e, i, o, y*, and *u* (but not *w* in
this case)—typically represent the sound of their letter names,
except for *y*, which represents the names of both of the letters *i* and
e. All six represent phonemes identified as short or unglided, the
medial sounds in *pat, pet, pit, pot*, and *putt*, and each of the first five
represent the second sound of the last, the /u/ as in *sun*. In combination with each other, with *w*, and the consonant cluster *gh*, they
represent each others' sounds as well as new phonemes.

a

The vowel letter *a* most frequently represents the sound /a/ as in
apple and, with descending frequency, the sounds /u/, /æ/, /ɑ/,
and /au/. The vowel letter *a* should be taught in this order of sound
frequency so that children can make an association between sounds
they possess and the vowel letter. Later, in the discussion of procedures, a *set for diversity* (to recognize that a letter or symbol
represents at least one other sound) is described as desirable for
even first-day activity.

1. The sound of *a* as in *apple* /a/ is found usually in monosyllabic
words ending in one or more consonants but also occurs in accented
syllables of multisyllabic words also ending in one or more consonants. Examples include such words as *bad, can*, and *pat*, as well
as *attack* and *adapt*. The *a* in words such as *expanse* or *flange*, which
end in *e*, is unaffected by the final *e*, even though the *e* is diacritic,
because the *e* relates to the adjacent consonants *s* and *g*. Only a few
exceptions to this diacritic rule, such as *change, strange, waste,
haste*, and *taste*, exist.

The vowel plus *ste*-ending words have been identified as special
grapho-phonemic patterns that could be taught separately. *a* before
l and *r* and a few others are also exceptions to this rule.

2. The sound of *a* as in *angel*, /æ/, the long or glided vowel, usually
occurs in words in which the vowel is followed by a single consonant
plus final *e* (vce words). The sound occurs in *cake, tame, lame, fate,
bade*, as well as in their derivatives, *caking, tamed, fated*. It is also
found in words such as *make-maker, bake-baker, rake-raking*,

and so on. The sound occurs in open stressed syllables such as the first syllable in the words *lady* and *vacant*.

3. The sound of *a* as in *arm*, /ɑ/, the second short sound of *a*, is usually found before *r* and in a few other words, such as *father, squad*, and *suave*. In some dialects, it is often considered as identical to the /o/ in *pot*. Examples include *car, far, tar, spar, mar, carbon, bartender, farther, tarry, sparring, art, farm*, and *barn*. Exceptions such as *bare* and *fare* are explained by the presence of the diacritic *e*, whereas others, such as *Harry, Larry, tarry, marry, carry, narrow*, and *narrate*, are explained by the fact that they contain a double *r*. Still other exceptions, such as *vary* and *wary*, can be explained by their position in the first open accented syllable. The sound /ɑ/, as in *arm*, is the most frequent of all *a*'s before *r* pronunciations with the exceptions relatively few in number.

4. The sound /au/ is the third short sound of *a* and is generally found before *l*, spelled *au* or *aw*, and often again referred to as an allophone of /o/. It often is written using the letter *o*, but only before *r*, in such words as *or, for, forest, oranges*, and *orchid*. The words *all, fall, ball, always, altogether, talk, walk, stalk, lawn, law, slaw, flaw, dawn, spawn*, and *draw* illustrate the sound and its spelling.

5. The fifth sound of the letter *a*, the /u/ in *above*, is the second most frequent sound represented by the letter. In a running word count, /a/, *apple*, appeared 1,536 times; /u/, *about*, 797; /æ/, *angel*, 650; /ɑ/, *arm*, 280; and /au/, *all*, 219. The letter *a* represents /u/ in unstressed open or closed syllables and may be found in all positions—initial, medial, and final. Examples include *alone, above, across, about*, the word *a* (5 of the 189 most frequently used words in print), *extra, canvas, breakfast, familiar, zebra, miracle, idea*, and *alphabet*.

Applicable Generalizations

GENERALIZATION: A single vowel followed by one or two consonants usually has an unglided (or short) sound but may also be glided (or long). Try the unglided sound first.

The above generalization eliminates the inadequacies of such separate generalizations as "vowels in open syllables are usually long" (only 31 percent true according to Burmeister's studies), "single vowels in accented one-syllable words are usually short"

(61 to 63 percent true—see Table 15, p. 108), "one vowel in the middle of a one-syllable word is usually short" (62 to 73 percent true—see Table 15), and others which similarly have low to moderate utility values. The generalization as stated eliminates as well the need to try to teach the young child what a syllable or accented syllable is. It recognizes the implicit information that if a vowel is not short, it is long, and applies to closed and open syllables and allows for a simple visual inspection and relies on instruction that produces a recognition of the major alternative correspondences of symbol with sound.

The generalization in this format is applicable to all six vowel letters, *a, e, i, o, y,* and *u,* and thus we will refer back to it rather than repeating it anew in a consideration of each vowel. It also applies to each of the three short sounds represented by the letter *a:* /a/, /ɑ/, and /au/. However, knowing that a vowel has an unglided sound is not enough to decode a word. In the case of the letter *a,* prior teaching to form the association between *a* with /a/, *a* before *r,* and *a* before *l* is necessary before the child can be expected to use the generalization in any meaningful way.

The phoneme /a/, however, is accounted for principally by two graphemes, the *a* in closed syllables and the *a-e* pattern. Words containing the *a-e* pattern include *have, advance, badge, chance, dance, glance, manse, lapse, relapse,* and *salve.* When the diacritic *e* generalizations following *v, c, g,* and *s* are learned, it can be seen that these words follow the generalization that vowels followed by one or two consonants are unglided. The few exceptions, *salve* and *halve* (where the *l* is silent), or *morale, locale,* and *caste* occur late in instruction and should be discussed as exceptions to the diacritic rules. *Giraffe,* on the other hand, may come as early as the first or second book in some materials and is an exception to the diacritic *e* rule also. The unusual spelling of *au* to represent /a/ in *laugh* and *aunt* (for those of us who pronounce it as /ant/) is found in only these two words, both of which should be taught as sight words.

The phoneme /ɑ/ is almost wholly accounted for by *a* before *r,* by the *a* in *father, squad,* or *suave,* at the end of words such as *pa, la, fa, papa, mama, drama, aha, aria, lava, saga,* and *plaza,* by *a-e* in *starve, large, barge, charge, carve, farce,* and *sparse,* in French loan words such as *mirage, garage, massage, montage,* and *sabotage,* and by *ea* in *heart, hearth,* and their derivatives.

Although the rule that *a* at the end of words usually sounds like /ɑ/ could be used, the *a-e* pattern representing /ɑ/ can be seen as following the *a* before *r* pattern when the diacritic *e* rules after *v, c, s,* and *g* are applied. Since almost all the situations where *ea* equals /ɑ/ relate to *heart* or *hearth*, sight-word development on these as they occur will account for all derivations.

The French loan words can be isolated, described as such, and the appropriate pronunciation given.

The graphemes *a* before *l, au,* and *aw* account for a little more than 40 percent of the instances of the phoneme /au/. Since this phoneme is often related to /o/, *dog,* and is not distinguished as a separate phoneme by some, it's not surprising that the letter *o* figures largely in the spellings representing /au/. In fact, the *o* before *r,* as in *or, horse,* and *cord,* accounts for almost 52 percent of the graphemes representing /au/. The *ough* in *thought, sought, fought, brought,* and *ought,* and the *augh* in *caught, daughter, taught, distraught, slaughter,* and *naughty,* each account for about 2 percent of the graphemes representing /au/.

The /au/ sound of *o* before *r* should be taught as a second short sound of *o* found usually before *r* in such words as *or, for, accord, adorn, corn, form, organ, forty,* or *horn.* Note, however, that *o* before *r* also represents /œ/ when followed by *e* (see below).

Based on the above, the graphemes *or, al, au,* and *aw* may be taught as usually representing the /au/ phoneme. The patterns *ough* and *augh,* however, should be taught in the context of the words in which they are found since, as seen earlier, *augh* also represents the phonemes /a/ and /f/ in *laugh,* and *ough* will be seen to represent /ou/, /œ/, and even /of/.

GENERALIZATION: When the vowel pairs *ai, ay, ee,* and *oa* are seen in a word, the first vowel usually represents its glided sound.

The generalization as stated is highly useful. Moreover, it is markedly different from the incorrect generalization that is often stated as "when two vowels go walking, the first does the talking." As shown by Clymer (1963), Bailey (1967), and Emans (1967), this generalization, which has been stated in the literature as "When there are two vowels together in a word, the first is usually long, and the second silent," had at best 45 percent utility and at worst 18 percent. As such, it should be rejected for use in instruction.

Burmeister (1968) modifies this generalization to add both *ea* and *ow* to the graphemes listed. However, she seems to ignore her own findings in doing so, for in her study "Vowel Pairs" (1968a) she reports that *ea* and *ow* represented the glided *e* and *o* sounds respectively only 50 to 60 percent of the time. This is hardly sufficient to warrant their inclusion.

This generalization should never be modified to "when two vowels go walking, . . ." and should be restricted to only four graphemes or spelling patterns. Many generations of children have been given incorrect information and we should not perpetuate ignorance today.

The *ai* and *ay* represented /æ/ 90 percent of the time they were found in the Hanna corpus, but *ai* represented the /æ/ only 71 percent of the time in the Dewey (1970) running-word corpus, where *ay* represented /æ/ 95 percent of the time. The words *said* and *again*, where *ai* represents /e/, account for much of this difference. So long as the exceptions *said, again, against, captain, mountain, certain, bargain, aisle, kayak,* and *bayou* are noted at the appropriate levels (*said* and *again* in the first grade, the other exceptions in second and third), little difficulty in applying this generalization to *ai* and *ay* in words should be experienced. The *ai* for /æ/ is found in *laid, paid, maid, main, vail, pail, raid, rain, wail, train, sail, daisy, daily, praise, raise, air, pair, fair, stair, chair, hair, fairy* (and in *straight* where *gh* is silent); the *ay* appears in *lay, may, day, stay, gray, pay, play, tray, way.*

The grapheme *ea* represents /æ/ in only a limited number of words, and in each case it is followed by *r*, as in *tear, wear, pear,* and *bear* and their derivatives. Since *ea* also represents the /ɑ/ in *heart,* the /ɛɛ/ in *ear,* and occasionally also the /u/ in *heard,* confusion can result. It can be avoided only by ensuring recognition of the grapheme *ea* in the context of the group of words to which it applies. Essentially, a level of sight recognition must be developed and a set for diversity to expect other pronunciations established. The use of context or the syntax of a sentence in which the words are used also helps in their correct identification and pronunciation, although context and syntax can be misleading.

The grapheme *eigh* represents the /æ/ in *eight, weigh, sleigh, neigh, neighbor,* and their derivatives, and *aigh* represents /æ/ in *straight* and its derivatives. Since *eigh* also represents /ie/ in *height* and *sleight,* care to distinguish between these should be taken.

The *ey* grapheme represents /æ/ in only a small number of words, such as *they, obey, convey, hey, prey,* and *survey.* The pattern *ey* to represent /æ/ will be established early since the word *they* will be used often and is ordinarily developed as a sight word. However, the correspondence of *th* with /ᵗh/ and *ey* with /æ/ may also be developed. Since *ey* equals /ɛɛ/ is the more frequent correspondence, the /æ/ pronunciation is an exception to a generalization for *y* and *ey* at the end of words (see *e*, below).

e

The vowel letter *e* represents the phonemes /e/, *Eskimo*, /ɛɛ/, *eagle*, /u/, *sun*, and /i/, *Indian*, in descending order of frequency and serves as a diacritic.

1. The letter *e* represents /e/, *Eskimo*, most often and, like *a*, can be predicted using the generalization that "a single vowel followed by one or two consonants may be unglided or glided. Try the unglided sound first." Examples include *red, bed, led, fed, sled, fled, bred, ebb, egg, edit, elf, elk, elm, end, exit, excite, closet, dogged, enjoy, affect, fresh, amen, bench, women, collect,* and *press.* In such words as *nonsense, else, edge, dense, delve, fence, pledge, shelve,* where a final *e* appears, the diacritic function of *e* after *c, g, s,* and *v* overrides, and the initial or medial *e* remains unglided or short.

The pattern *ea*, representing /e/ in 3 percent of its usages, is commonly found in such words as *read* (past tense), *head, dead, heavy, breath, meant, treasure, spread, wealth, feather, health, pleasant, breakfast,* and their derivatives. Some of these can be taught as sight words, but the contrast procedure, as shown below, is recommended to develop the association of the pattern and the sounds it represents. The contrast with words where the *ea* represents the glided vowel, as in *eagle,* is used to help the child recognize which words contain the unglided *e* and which contain the glided *e*.

The pattern *e-e*, representing /e/ in 3 percent of its usages, is found in words ending in *s, g, c,* and *v* plus *e* where the diacritic is overriding. Examples include *edge, else, college, sense, shelve, tense, twelve, whence, commence, hence,* and *fence.* A recognition of the use of the diacritic with such words allows a further recognition that this group of words follows the generalization on page 82, and the pattern *e-e* can be eliminated from the listing in Table 11.

2. The sound of *e* in *eagle,* the name sound of the letter, is most often represented by *y* in final positions of words; by *ee*, for which the vowel-pairs generalization applies; by *e*, for which the generalizations on pages 82 and 87 apply; by *e-e*, for which the diacritic generalization on page 80 applies; by *ea, ie, i-e, ei,* and also *ey.*

The grapheme *ee* is found in such words as *see, tree, queen, feel, peel, meet,* and *street,* and the grapheme *ea* is found in such words as *lead* (verb), *bead, read* (verb), *sea, tea, ease, leaf, eager, eagle, speak, weak, deal, meal, clean, mean, peace, please, easel, reason, season, meat,* and *leave.* Since *ea* represents the glided *e* only 64 percent of the time, unlike *ai, ay, ee,* or *oa,* which have frequencies over 90 percent, its inclusion in this generalization is not warranted. A listing and pronunciation of the words noted above, where *ea* represents the glided sound, might be used to recognize its moderate regularity. It might then be contrasted with a list of words in which the *ea* represents the unglided *e,* the glided *a,* and the schwa.

The grapheme *e* as found in *be, he, she, me* is identified using the generalization "if the only vowel letter is at the end of a two- or three-letter word, the vowel usually represents a glided (or long) sound." The single letter *e* in words such as *even, female, lever,* or *meter* is accounted for by the generalization for "a single vowel followed by one or two consonants. . . ."

The graphemes *ie* and *i-e* follow the diacritic generalizations on pages 79 and 80, indicating that adjacent vowel or vowels once-removed are glided. However, some difficulty will occur in using the generalizations until it is also recognized that the fourth sound of *i* is /ee/ (see *i,* below). The grapheme *ie* is typically found at the end of such words as *birdie, brownie, caddie, collie, laddie,* and *lassie,* where it is used as a diminutive. The pattern is constructed where we "change *y* to *i* and add *es* or *ed*" in *hurry-hurried, candy-candies, marry-marries-married,* and the like. It is also found in *movie, prairie, genie, reverie,* and *calorie.* An alternative spelling of the /ee/ sound in many of these words is *y,* which again represents the /ee/ sound. Examples include *laddy, caddy, calory.*

GENERALIZATION: *y* and *ey* at the end of words usually represent /ee/, but *y* can also represent /ie/. Try the /ee/ sound first.

This generalization has high utility and permits decoding of *y-* and *ey*-ending words with relative ease. As discussed in Chapter 1, *y* and *ey* are often identified as representing the phoneme /i/, as in *Indian,* yet as Dewey (1970:14) points out the phoneme has the quality of /ee/ with the shortness of /i/. Identified as the schwi sound to correspond with the schwa, both of which are the unstressed phonemes /ee/ and /u/, the /ee/ sound is used by children and adults in their own writing when the actual spelling is unknown. There is no reason, therefore, to continue to follow an antique custom of phoneticians or lexicographers. (Note that the editors of Webster's

Third New International Dictionary use the pronunciation long *e* in such unaccented syllables.)

The pattern *ei* representing /ϵϵ/ occurs only a small percentage of the time to represent this phoneme, and it may be mispronounced since it appears in *reign, rein, vein,* and *heir,* where it represents /æ/, and in *forfeit, foreign,* and *counterfeit,* where it represents /i/. Its most frequent usage, however, is to represent the /ϵϵ/ phoneme. It is found in such words as *weird, ceiling, receipt, deceit, sheik, either, neither, seizure, receive,* and *seize.* Since *either* and *neither* often appear in children's materials, the pattern cannot be ignored. Neither should the incorrect "two vowel" rule be suggested as applicable. To develop the pattern, use a chalkboard on which are listed the words to which it applies and the words to which it does not apply.

3. The phoneme /u/, represented by the letter *e* 24 percent of the time, is the third most frequent sound of the letter and is usually identified as the schwa sound since it occurs in unstressed open or closed syllables. It can be identified in the words *fallen, awaken, novel, level, vowel, agent, counsel, darken, science, intelligence,* and so on. In words containing two vowel phonemes, the /u/ sound is usually represented by the *e* in the last part of the word. In words containing three or more vowels, the *e* also represents /u/ in the last part of the word when we note that final *e* is a diacritic and silent. (See *u,* below.)

4. The fourth sound of *e,* /i/, *Indian,* is found only rarely and is seen in such words as *pretty, prettily,* and *privilege.* It is also represented by *ei,* as in *counterfeit* or *foreign,* and by double *e,* as in *been* and *breeches.*

i

The letter *i* represents the phonemes /i/, *Indian,* /ie/, *ice,* and /u/, *sun,* but its principal uses are to represent the regular unglided and glided sounds of the vowel.

1. The unglided sound of the vowel, /i/, *Indian,* is the most frequent of all the vowel sounds and should be taught first in a sequence. It can be identified using the generalization that "a single vowel followed by one or two consonants usually has an unglided . . . ." It is found in such words as *sit, bit, bin, kin, win, wit, knit, thing, miss, admit, distinct, dig,* and *dignity.*

The second most frequent spelling of /i/, *Indian,* is the letter *y,* which, like *i* can be decoded using the same generalization, as in *gym, gypsy, hymn, hypnotize, myth, pygmy, syllable, symbol, symptom, symphony, typical, bicycle, mystery,* and *synthetic.*

The third most frequent spelling, *i-e,* is found in such words as *massive, alive, forgive, bridge, cringe, hinge, glimpse, promise, eclipse, since, wince, prince, office,* and *notice.* Using diacritic *e* rules related to *e* after *c, v, g* and *s,* the *i* can be seen to be decodable from the same generalization. The occasional exception, such as *grille,* points up the fact that *e* occasionally has no diacritic function owing to the addition of French loan words to the language.

The *a-e* pattern in such words as *voyage, manage, cabbage, postage, bandage, furnace, necklace, surface, climate, chocolate,* and *private* indicates the ubiquitous role of the diacritic *e* after *s* and *g* in these cases. But it also indicates its purely graphic uses in *ate*-ending words. The fact that the letter *a* is used to represent the phoneme /i/, *Indian,* in 2 percent of this group of words would need to be called to the attention of children only when given words like *chocolate* and *cabbage* appear in early materials. It can be expanded upon in third- or fourth-level reading materials.

ui in *build* and *built* and their derivatives is a minor pattern and should be taught directly and in contrast to *fruit* and *suit.*

2. The phoneme /ie/, represented by *i* and *y* 88.4 percent of the time, can be decoded using the generalization for "a single vowel followed by one or two consonants . . . ," the generalization for "*y* at the end of words . . . ," the generalization for the patterns *i-e* and *y-e,* and the generalization for the pattern *ie.*

Words containing the letters *i* and *y* include *child, kind, find, bind, climb, design, diner, liken, sign, spicy, stylish, hydrant, dynamic, psychology, python, slay, why, try, my, dry, cry, deny, shy, sky, occupy, multiply,* and *modify.*

Words containing the *ie, i-e,* and *y-e* patterns include *tie, lie, pie, die, necktie, magpie,* as well as *cried, dried, fried, applied,* where the final *y* is changed to *i* before the morpheme *ed,* and *kite, side, knife, crime, file, five, dime, hike, hide, life, mile, wide, shine, time, lyre, rhyme, style, type, thyme.*

In words such as *size, dire, admire, advice, dime, arise, price, wise, vise, wither, lithe,* the diacritic *e* is sometimes said to signal information about the adjacent consonants as well as the preceding vowel. Since the generalization for "a single vowel followed by one or two consonants . . ." accounts for the glided vowel sound, the effect of the diacritic *e* on the vowel is superfluous. If it is emphasized that the *e* represents two signals, it may lead to incorrect pronunciations of *give* and the like.

The pattern *igh* in *high, might, night, tight, light, right,* and *fight* can also be taught as representing /ie/, but the generalization for "a single vowel . . ." decodes the sound. To reduce the number of tasks to be learned, this generalization could be discussed in relation to this group of words. In this way, recognition of the pattern and the use of the generalization would be achieved simultaneously.

o

The letter *o* represents the sounds /o/, *dog,* /œ/, *boat,* /u/, *sun,* /ω/, *book,* /ɷ/, *shoe,* and /au/, *auto,* but, as with all the unglided vowels discussed thus far, it represents the unglided sound, /o/, *dog,* most frequently. Table 14 demonstrates that over 1,800 occurrences of the three phonemes /o/, /ɑ/, and /au/ existed in the Dewey (1970) corpus, with /o/ predominating. A great number of speakers do discriminate between these three phonemes. This is done with relative ease when the following criteria are applied: /o/ wherever the single vowel is typically found; /ɑ/ before *r;* /au/ before *l, ll,* and when spelled *au* and *aw.* This suggests that these differences should be maintained to allow for regional differences in pronunciation.

1. The unglided sound /o/, *dog,* is represented by three graphemes *(o, a, o-e),* which, together, account for 99 percent of that phoneme's use in discourse. As shown in Table 10, the letter *o* by itself accounts for most of these usages (93 percent). /o/ is often related to /ɑ/ or /au/, and regional or local pronunciations may differ. The key word, *dog,* may be pronounced /dog/, /ḍ ɑ g/, or even /ḍaug/. While I've chosen to discriminate between all three, the teacher may relate this phoneme to the predominant local pronunciation.

TABLE 14. Occurrence and Graphemes of the Phonemes /o/, /ɑ/, and /au/

Phoneme	Occurrences in Words	Percentage of Grapheme Occurrences
/o/	1,103	o (92.6), a (3.2), o-e (1.9)
/ɑ/	332	a (87.0), a-e (6.8), ea (3.4)
/au/	442	o (49.5), a (24.2), a-e (2.3), au (8.6), aw (7.7), ough (2.0), augh (1.8)

Information related to /au/ in Table 12 is relevant, as is that related to the usage of *a* before *l*, *aw*, and *au*.

The letter *o* for /o/ is seen in *on, top, pot, lot, rot, got, off, body, clog, clot, cod, cob, cocky, comic, conduct* (noun), *copy, dock, clock, fog, follows, dollar, sock, sorry, stop, Amazon, monster,* and *spot*. It can be decoded using the generalization for "a single vowel followed by one or two consonants."

Want and *what* illustrate the uses of *a* to represent /o/ and, with their derivatives, constitute a large part of this usage. The *a* in *water* is pronounced /o/ about equally with /au/, whereas in *father* it alternates between /o/ and /a/.

The *o-e* pattern for /o/ in such words as *gone, begone, forgone,* and *bygone* illustrates that the diacritic *e* has no function here and thus a few words are exceptions to the regular application. The word *gone* when taught as a sight word accounts for the other three words in the list.

2. The glided vowel /œ/ in *go, no, phone, lone, shows, below, goat, boat, soul, shoulder, toe,* and *hoe* illustrates the frequency in which the various spellings *o, o-e, ow, oa, ou,* and *oe* represent the sound. It may be misleading to view the words *go* and *no* as illustrations of the sound since the letter *o* represents the sound /œ/ only occasionally at the end of short words. Its usage in initial and medial positions can be seen in such words as *most, old, only, folk, ghost, gross, coping, bony, noted, rogue, clothes, roll, comb, gold, coconut, cold, cozy, frozen, post, holy,* and so on. But the sound is also present in *ford, fort, worn, export, forth*. In all the cases cited except *go* and *no*, the /œ/ represented by *o* follows the generalization for "a single vowel. . . . " The generalization "if the only vowel letter is at the end of a two- or three-letter word, . . . " accounts for the words *go, no,* and so forth.

The pattern *o-e* in *bone, phone, lone, ode, ore, hope, woke, cone, bone, choke, cope, demote, denote, home, pole, stove, scope, sole, snore,* and *throne* can be decoded using the diacritic *e* generalization. A few words like *cove, stove, grove, dove, close, nose, doze,* and *rose* exist among the many *o-e* words where diacritic rules for *v*, *s*, and *z* act also to signal the /œ/ sound of the preceding vowel.

The *oe* pattern in *toe, hoe, roe,* and *woe* can be decoded using the generalization for "*e* following a vowel at the end of a word. . . ." The *oa* in *goat, boat, float, throat, load, croak,* and *soap* can be decoded using the two-vowel generalization. As with *ea*, previously discussed, the temptation to add *ow* to this generalization should be rigorously suppressed since *ow* represents the glided *o*, as in *show, know,* and *throw,* only a little better than 51 percent of the time among 243 words in the Hanna corpus—hardly better than chance. Such words as *own, bowl, know, bow, row, show, growth,* and *thrown,* in which the *ow* represents the glided vowel, can be contrasted with words in which the *ow* represents the glided vowel /œ/, *now, how, row, bow, brown, clown, crowd, down, town,* to bring about the association of the grapheme with its phonemes.

The *ou* pattern, in *soul, shoulder, poultry,* and *mould,* presents a problem in decoding since the *ou* represents a variety of phonemes (/œ/, /ou/, /u/, /ω/, /ω/, /au/). Its most frequent usage is to represent the /ou/, *owl,* phoneme. Contrasting *ou* as /oe/ words with words in which *ou* represents another phoneme appears to be a good way to associate graphemes with phonemes.

The pattern *ough* in *though, dough, borough, furlough,* and *although,* not listed among the graphemes necessary to achieve 97 percent decoding success with the phoneme /œ/, is a minor pattern representing the phoneme in only eight words of the Hanna 17,310-word corpus. Since we often use *though* and *although,* the minor pattern cannot be ignored. Those two words can be taught as sight words and related to the others as they appear, or developed contrastively with others that also use the *ough* pattern.

3. The third most frequent sound represented by *o* is /u/. As seen below, *o* is used almost as frequently as *u* to represent this sound. Like the *a, e,* and *i, o* represents the sound in unaccented syllables in such words as *bottom, crayon, dragon, lemon, mammoth, method, period, ration, ribbon, wagon, vision, addition, subtraction, apron, bacon, canyon, melon, carton, collect, condense, complete, diamond, demon, idol, symbol,* and *wisdom.* Teaching the child that *o* represents three sounds at initial stages of reading acquisition is an important task. It is supplemented by later instruction on accent or stress.

4. The fourth sound represented by *o* is /ω/ as in *woman, bosom,* or *wolf. o* is one of the least frequent of the spellings used to represent the sound. It also occurs in the word *to,* as pronounced in the phrase *to go,* where *to* is unstressed, and in the words *today, tonight, tomorrow,* and *altogether.* These words should be isolated on a chalkboard list for discussion and association. Comment such as, "the word *to* in isolation or by itself sounds one way but in speech or in words such as the word *to* or that part of the word in *today* and *tomorrow* is pronounced differently /tω/," will help the child in

decoding appropriately. If the first syllable in *today* in decoding activity is stressed by anyone, the pronunciation will be seen to relate to the more frequent usage of /tᴚ/ for *to* in isolation and will not interfere with communication.

The /ᴚ/ phoneme is also spelled as *oo, ou, u,* and *u-e* as well as *o*. Together these five spellings represent /ᴚ/ 99.7 percent of the time in print. Often the number of words to illustrate each spelling is small, and only 368 words were found in the Hanna corpus.

The second most frequent spelling of /ᴚ/, *book,* is *oo,* the unglided sound of the vowel pair /ᴚ/-/ᴚ/, *book-food*. When the pattern *oo,* like *gh, th, sh,* or *ph* is learned as one grapheme representing a phoneme ("We don't have enough single letters in our alphabet to represent all of the sounds of speech and so some combination of letters are used to represent some sounds. These combinations— *ph, oo, gh, sh, ch,* and *th*—are usually thought of as one combination letter [or grapheme]."), the *oo* represents an unglided and a glided vowel sound. The unglided and glided sounds are decodable using the generalization for "a single vowel followed by one or two consonants. . . ," with the unglided sound the more frequent one. The unglided sound of *oo* is found in *book, cook, crook, foot, brook, good, hood, look, moor, poor, shook, soot, stood, wood, wool,* in the compounds *barefoot, cookbook, fishhook, outlook, boyhood,* and in derivatives such as *woody, woolen,* and *mooring.*

The letter *u,* representing /ᴚ/, is seen in *bull, bullet, bush, full, jury, pull, push, sugar,* and in the *ful* endings of such words as *armful, beautiful, harmful, playful,* and *peaceful.* It is the most frequent spelling for the /ᴚ/ phoneme and as such represents a third phoneme represented by the letter *u*. As an unglided vowel, it can be decoded using the generalization for "a single vowel followed by one or two consonants," but this can be used only when the *u* is identified as representing two unglided phonemes and the rule of flexibility in moving from one sound to the next is followed.

The grapheme *u-e,* in *sure, brochure, insure,* and *reassure,* is seen to follow the same generalization for single vowels when the generalization for diacritic *e* is applied to consonants once-removed. The pattern is so infrequent, however, that the word *sure* should be learned as a sight word.

5. The fifth phoneme represented by *o,* that of /ᴚ/, *shoe,* represents that sound in *tomb, whom, who, do, approval, loser, movie,* and *two*. At the end of words, *o,* like *e, i* and *y,* most often represents

a glided vowel sound, whereas *a* represents the unglided sound /ɑ/, and *u* appears at the end of words only in combination with another vowel to represent /ω/. The following generalization applies to the vowel *o* representing /ω/ in this case:

GENERALIZATION: If the only vowel letter is at the end of a two- or three-letter word, the letter usually represents a glided vowel sound.

Since the letter *o* represents both the glided and unglided sounds /œ/ and /o/ as well as /ω/ and /ω/, it would be only natural that children might say /dœ/ instead of /dω/ for the spelling *do*. So long as children are taught the variety of sounds that letters represent, they should move from the first to the second glided sound of the vowel letter to decode such words. Grouping of such /ω/ words on the chalkboard and contrasting this pronunciation with that of /œ/ in such words as *go, no,* and *so* is a procedure that should be used to help children recognize which words belong in each group.

The phoneme /ω/, represented about 8 percent of the time by *o*, is also represented by *oo, u, ou, u-e, ew, ue,* and *o-e,* a total of eight graphemes in all for a decoding capability of a little more than 94 percent. The word *shoe,* used to illustrate the sound, might be thought of as a ninth pattern, and *oo-e* in *ooze,* as a tenth pattern. Since *e* acts as a diacritic, the *o* in shoe is accounted for by diacritic *e* "following a vowel at the end of words." The *oo* in *ooze* is included with *oo* patterns since the *e* is a diacritic referring to *z*.

The *oo* grapheme as described above under /ω/ stands for its glided sound in such words as *noon, balloon, bloom, booth, boot, brood, doom, gloom, maroon, roof, roost, shoot, tooth, proof,* and in such compounds as *ballroom, fireproof, redwood, toadstool,* and *mushroom*. It follows the generalization for single vowels as noted earlier for /ω/. At the end of *coo, zoo, too, taboo, shampoo, boo, woo,* and *tattoo,* the *oo* pattern is decodable using the generalization for "the only vowel letter at the end of a short word."

The letter *u* represents the unglided sound /ω/ and the glided vowel sound /ω/. The /ω/ phoneme is found in such words as *brutish, plumage, truth, crucial, cruel, hula, junior, ruby, truant, tuna,* and *crusade*. Although *u* as /ω/ can be decoded from the generalization for "a single vowel followed by one or two consonants . . . ," contrast procedures should also be followed since *u* represents /ω/ and /ω/ as well as /u/ and /ue/. A grouping listed under the symbol to represent its sound should be made to help the child recognize which words are pronounced in which way.

The grapheme *ou* represents the unglided sound /ω/ a little more frequently than the glided sound /ō/. This follows a consistent pattern for all the vowel letters except *y*, as discussed below. The pattern *ou* for /ō/ appears in only a small group of words, including *group, soup, wound, youth, coupon, bouquet, rouge,* and *route,* as well as *you, bayou,* and *through.* Again, the generalization for "a single vowel followed by one or two consonants" applies to the words *group* to *route,* but the presence of the diacritic *e* is purely graphic, an exception. The generalization for "the only vowel letter at the end of a short word" applies to *you, bayou,* and *sou,* while *through* and *throughout* alone use the *ough* grapheme for /ō/. For reasons of efficiency, *through* should be taught as a sight word along with *you* at an early point, since the usages are too few to spend time on in applying generalizations.

The grapheme *u-e* in *brute, exclude, flute, prude, prune, rude, rule,* and *yule* follows the generalization for "*e* following a vowel and consonant," whereas *ue* in such words as *blue, clue, glue, flue,* and *true* follows the generalization for "*e* following a vowel at the end of words." The grapheme *ew* is one of the few vowel digraphs in which *o* or *u* do not figure and yet represents the phoneme /ō/. *o* and *u* have a relational history and alternate with each other in representing a number of phonemes, but *ew* is completely deviant in this sense. The *ew* is found in *blew, chew, crew, drew, flew, grew, new, jewel,* and *screw,* as well as *shrewd* and *strewn.* Although the glided sound of the vowel is represented here principally at the end of words, no generalization applies. The pattern *ew* must be taught to correspond with /ō/ for the limited number of words (twenty-two) in which it is found. After *r, ch, l,* and *j, ew* corresponds to /ω/.

The *o-e* pattern in *move, approve, lose,* and *whose* is not a new pattern. The diacritic *e* after *v* and *s* applies and *o* follows the generalization for "a single vowel followed by one or two consonants." It belongs to the earlier category representing /ω/.

The Digraph /oi/

A special category has been established for /oi/ and /ou/ since neither have a single vowel letter to represent them. The word "digraph" applies because the phoneme is identified by two letters.

oi represents the glided phoneme /ȯi/ as in *oil* or *oyster*. All its usages include either the *oi* or the *oy* spelling. No generalization applies to this pattern except the associational one that *oi* and *oy* represent the phoneme /ȯi/ as seen in *oil, boil, toil, foil, soil, broil, noise, foist, quoit, point, loin, poison, choice,* and *noise,* and in *boy, convoy, coy, destroy, employ, loyal, toy,* and *voyage.* Notice diacritic *e* after *c* and *s* in *noise, voice,* and *choice.*

The Digraph /ȯu/

The digraph /ȯu/ is represented typically by either *ou* or *ow* and, as with /ȯi/, the patterns must often be taught directly. The *ou,* as seen in *out, hour, our, house, bound, about, account, aloud, round, cloud, doubt, count, found, flour, mouth, ground, proud, south, thousand,* and *trouser,* consistently appears in initial or medial positions except for the word *thou.* Like /ȯi/, it is a glided vowel and the generalization for "a single vowel followed by one or two consonants" applies. It has no unglided counterpart. Thus, it is more desirable to teach the pattern directly, contrasting it with *could, would,* and *should,* where it represents /ᴡ/. Pattern teaching holds also for *mouse, house, spouse, announce, flounce, pounce,* and *lounge,* where the diacritic *e* functions in regard to *s, c,* and *g.*

The *ow* pattern also represents /ȯu/ as in *brown, clown, crowd, down, town, fowl, frown, gown, growl, howl, allow, brow, bow, chow, chowder, cow, how, now, flower, plowman, power, prow, row, sow, towel,* and *vowel.* Such look-alikes as *bow,* /bȯu/, /bōe/, and *row,* /rȯu/, /rōe/, need special attention since only contextual usage can distinguish between them.

The words *drought, bough,* and *slough* illustrate the same kind of confusion, possibly because *ough* is used to represent /au/ in *ought* and *bought* and /ōe/ in *dough.* The pattern of *ough* for /ȯu/ is found in only four words and should be developed as a contrast and in direct association as the words appear in children's materials.

y

The letter *y,* the fifth vowel letter in terms of usage in representing vowel sounds, represents the vowel phonemes /ᴇ̄/, /ie/, /i/, and /u/ and the consonant phoneme /y/. The consonant usage (about 3 percent of the time) has been discussed with other consonants (see p. 67), and the usages of *y* to represent /i/, /ᴇ̄/, and /ie/ have been discussed above under the letters *e* and *i*. The use of *y* to represent /u/ is infrequent, and that usage is before *r*, as in *myrtle* and *myrrh*, and in unaccented syllables such as in the words *idyll, ethyl, methyl, synonymous,* or *oxygen.* Since the pattern is of minor concern, *myrtle* and *myrrh* would best be taught as sight words as they occur; the pronunciation of the other words could be supplied as the words appear at later levels in science or English materials. Yet the generalization on page 98, vowels before *l, m, n,* and *r* in the last part of words, applies to *y,* as seen in *ethyl, idyll,* and *methyl.*

u

The letter *u* represents the unglided and glided phonemes /u/, *sun,* and /ue/, *unite,* about 59 percent of the time that the single letter is used in such words as *sun, but, fun, rut, spun, sputter, cup, rub, bubble, unite, union, human, accurate, argue, cute, use, unit, value,* and *vocabulary.* The single letter *u* also represents /ꙩ/ and /ꙩ/ in such words as *flute, salute, blue, assume, tutor, spruce, truth, virtue, reduce, dude, due, duke, during, flu, fluid, bushel, bullet, full, cushion, pull, bull, bush, sure, sugar, put, push,* and *pussy,* and in the morpheme *ful* in *awful, beautiful, hateful, joyful,* and the like.

The letter *u* also represents the consonant sound /w/, as in *quiet, queen, quill, quick,* in about 6 percent of its usage. It acts as a diacritic with no sound value in about 1 percent of its usage to separate *g* from *e* or *i* in *tongue, guess, league, guide, guilt, guild,* and *guitar.* It is silent in *que*-endings of French loan words, follows *o* and *a* to represent a variety of phonemes in 22 percent of its usage, and combines with *i, e, y* or *ea* to represent other phonemes about 1 percent of the time. In short, the letter *u* is the most variable of all vowel letters in its usages.

The phoneme /u/ seen represented by *o* in *mother* is often distinguished as different from the phoneme represented by the *e* in that the *o* in *mother* represents /u/ in a stressed position, whereas the *e* represents /u/ in an unstressed position. But, as indicated in Chapter 2, such fine distinctions are excellent for phoneticians but of no importance in the practical situation of reading instruction.

The letters *a* and *e* represent the phoneme /u/, more often than *u,* and the sound is also represented by *o, i,* the digraph *ou,* and the patterns *o-e, a-e,* and *ea.*

Of first interest is the letter *u* representing the unglided sound of the vowel /u/, *sun.* The generalization for "a single vowel followed by one or two consonants" applies in all uses of *u* as /u/.

a *as* /u/

As indicated by its percentage of usage (25.2 percent) in Table 10, the letter *a* represents the /u/ phoneme more often than any other in printed discourse. The primary reason for this is the very frequent use of the words *a*, *an*, and *and* in their unstressed versions. The letter *a*, for example, when used before a consonant, most often represents /u/, rather than its letter name. When *an* is used before vowels and words beginning with *h*, the pronunciation is likely to be /un/. The word *and*, often described as syllabic *n*, represents a reduced or unstressed /u/ sound followed by /n/ in such phrases as *ham 'n eggs, bread 'n butter, sugar 'n milk*, where the phoneme /d/ in *and* is often omitted. Since these three words, *a, an, and*, are used so often, their more frequent pronunciations should be taught directly, as indicated in Chapter 5, for the word *a*, establishing a set for diversity in initial instruction.

Since, in early instruction, it is not desirable to refer to syllabication or stress, decoding of the letter *a* to /u/ is often difficult. When the generalization for "a single vowel followed by one or two consonants" is introduced and then used by children, a distortion of the sound normally heard in speech will be produced. However, when the usual pronunciation, /u/, is encouraged, adjustment will often be rapid. There is a general rule, however, which can be taught for identifying the /u/ *sound of a (e, i,* and *o)* in the second, third, and final syllables of words:

GENERALIZATION: The vowels *a, e, i, o,* and *y* followed by *l, m, n,* or *r* in the last part of words having two or more vowel sounds are usually pronounced /u/.

The rule derives from the tendency of speakers to produce the syllabic *n, m, l,* or *r* in many words. In the case of the letter *a*, it can be seen to be applicable to *madam, Adam, animal, bridal, equal, fatal, metal, total, local, special, postman, workman, England, husband, beggar, collar, mustard, orchard, regular,* and *standard*. This generalization, however, does not account for all instances of *a* for /u/, since the unstressed /u/, or schwa sound, is found in initial and medial position of words before other letters. In such frequently used words in beginning materials (as well as in speech and print) as *above, alone, across, against,* and *among*, the letter *a* represents /u/ (an exception is *after*). Although this could be explained at a later point on the basis of unstressed syllables, it is desirable, when developing such sight words, to point out that the second short sound of *a* is /u/ in many words; and that, since in a list of 335 words beginning with *a*, the letter *a* represented the /u/ sound almost 80 percent of the time, at the beginning of words the letter *a* most often stands for /u/.

The letter *a* in medial positions, whether singly as a syllable or as part of a syllable, can only be decoded using stress rules for multisyllabic words. Such rules for usage at later levels are given below. When such usages arise, sound approximation using the generalization for "a single vowel followed by one or two consonants," with adjustment by familiarity with the word, must be relied on.

The pattern *a-e*, as in *pirate* or *purchase*, is restricted to a few words and need not be dwelt on except to note that the diacritic *e* is silent, being purely graphical in *pirate* and indicates the /s/ pronunciation in *purchase*. Other words ending in *a-e*, such as *Senate, private, climate, accurate, chocolate, fortunate, palate, estimate* (noun), and *separate* (adjective), have the unglided /i/ sound but may also be /u/ in some pronunciations. However, the *American College Dictionary* (1961), Webster's *Third New International Dictionary* (1963), and *The Random House Dictionary* (1967) indicate that the *a* represents /i/ in such words.

An analysis of the word corpuses for the letter *e* pronounced /u/ indicates that *e* followed by *l, m, n,* and *r* in the last part of such words as *barrel, cruel, jewel, camel, scoundrel, system, solemn, tandem, spoken, woven, legend, sunken, waken, evident, compliment, expert, concert, inert, insert, transfer,* and after *r* in any position *(her, fervor, germ, herd, mercy, perfect, person)* accounts for over 90 percent of this usage. The generalization on p. 98 for "the vowels *a, e, i,* and *o* followed by *l, m, n,* or *r* . . ." should certainly be used to help children reduce uncertainty about which sound the letter *e* represents.

The letter *e* is rarely, if ever, used in the initial position or first syllable of multisyllabic words to represent /u/.

The letter *o*, like *e* when followed by *m, n,* or *l* at the end of words, usually represents /u/ in most two- and three-syllable words, as in *bottom, dragon, boredom, wagon, pistol, carol, idol, vitriol, viol, gambol* (an exception is *control*), where stress is on the first or second syllable. The letter *o* before *r* in two- and three-syllable words such as *author, auditor, possessor, professor, oppressor, color, honor, favor, harbor, labor, major, doctor, factor,* and *horror* also represents the /u/ sound. The generalization on p. 98 for the vowels *a, e, i,* and *o* followed by *l, m, n,* or *r* . . . is useful in decoding such endings.

The letter *o* (and the pattern *o-e* in *worse,* which corresponds to *o* when the diacritic *e* after *s* is recognized) represents the /u/ phoneme when followed by *r* in such one-syllable words as *work, word, world, worry, worship, worst, worth, worm,* their derivatives, when appropriate, and *attorney, borough,* and *whorl.* Since *o* before *r* usually represents /œ/ or /au/, this group of words should be isolated for grapheme-phoneme association rather than for application of any generalization.

The /u/ phoneme is also represented by *o* in the endings *some* and *come* in such compounds as *wholesome, lonesome,* and *welcome.* Here, the diacritic *e* has no value. In the words *some* or *come,* the /u/ phoneme also exists. Unfortunately, for such initial uses as the *o* has in *object,* /object/, and *objective,* /ubjective/, stress must be considered.

The /u/ phoneme, represented by *a, e, i, o,* and *y,* is found in unstressed syllables and is ambiguous. As long as it is possible to recognize which part of a word is stressed, it is possible to instruct that the short sound represented by any vowel letter is usually /u/. Stress is not indicated by our print system, but we can point out that

1. If *a, in, re, ex, de,* or *be* appear as the first part of a word containing another vowel grapheme, the first part is usually unstressed.
2. In most two-syllable words, the first syllable is stressed.
3. When there are double consonants within a word, the vowel before the double consonant is usually stressed.
4. Two vowel letters together in the last part of a word is often a clue to a stressed final syllable.

e and *o* in such words as *decide, between, convey, complain,* and *conceal* follow these rules of stress. Use of the generalization for single vowels will obtain a pronunciation that approximates the correct sound; this is usually followed by an adjustment on the reader's part to the correct sound when the decoded word is familiar.

The letters *ou* followed by *s* at the end of a word always represent /u/, as in *curious, envious, jealous, delicious, joyous, glorious, furious, voracious, courageous, unconscious, mischievous,* and *atrocious.*

The pattern *ou* also represents /u/ before *r* in *adjourn, courage, courtesy, discourage, flourish, nourish,* and *scourge* but not in *hour, our, ourself,* and *ourselves* and rarely in other positions. The patterns *ous* and *our* should be taught directly since no generalization is necessary for so few words.

The letter *i* also represents the sound /u/ in unstressed syllables before *l, n,* and *m,* as seen in *basin, raisin, Latin, satin, civil, peril, basil, nostril, stencil, fragile, fertile, medicine, missile,* and before *r* in *elixir, tapir, Hampshire,* and *Yorkshire. i* before *r* in *bird, circus, virtue, fir, stir, squirrel, sir, admiral, aspirin,* and *perspiration* also illustrates the /u/ pronunciation of *i* before *r* as noted under *i* in accented and unaccented syllables. The generalization for vowels before *l, m, n,* and *r,* in the last part of words can be amended to include *i.*

The pattern *ea* represents the /u/ sound in stressed syllables before *r* in such words as *early, earn, earth, heard, learn, pearl, search,* and *rehearse,* and before *n* at the end of words such as *sergeant* and *pageant.* As noted in Table 10, *ea* contributes less than 1 percent to a decoding of the /u/ sound in print; and, as seen above, it follows the generalization for "vowels followed by *l, m, n,* or *r*" only in the case of *n.* It should be taught as a pattern in the words listed.

The letter *u* represents the /ue/ phoneme only a very small percent of the time. The phoneme /ue/ is also one of the least frequently used phonemes in discourse and is supplanted by /ထ/ in many words. In the Rinsland *Basic Vocabulary List,* only 155 words were found in which the letter *u* represented /ue/. This occurred in such words as *cute, argue, human, union, use, excuse, cupid, cubic, tulip, pupil, music, usual,* and *student.* Since pronunciations of *during, duty, supervisor,* and others alternate between /ue/ and /ထ/ in American speech, the teacher should use caution in selecting words for use in chalkboard or duplicated exercises. If the teacher develops an association of symbol with sound and encourages the use of the generalization for "a single vowel followed by one or two consonants," the sound /ue/ will, after /u/, be decoded by children. Moreover, they will adjust their pronunciation to express whichever sound they find in agreement with a known word in their vocabulary or as pronounced by the teacher.

The pattern *u-e* in *cube, acute, failure, cure, fume, tribute, use,* and *pure,* and *ue* in *cue, hue, avenue, value,* representing /ue/, are decodable using the generalizations for "*e* following a vowel at the end of a word" and "*e* following a vowel and a consonant," respectively. As with *u,* the patterns *u-e* and *ue* in such words as *rule, due, sue, tune, issue,* and *statue* may alternatively represent /ue/ or /ထ/

in some areas. The teacher should choose the local pronunciation to illustrate the use of these generalizations and should expect the child to use either his or her own pronunciation or the one used by teachers and peers.

The grapheme *ew* represents /ue/ in some but not all pronunciations of *new, knew, dew, few, hew, pew, sewage, curfew, mildew, nephew,* and *stew.* Another pronunciation for *ew* in *new, knew, mildew,* and *stew* is /ထ/. As indicated above for /ထ/, the pattern *ew* is a rare one, and after *r, l, ch,* and *j,* the phoneme is usually /ထ/. As with all other consonants, *ew* as /ue/ is a consistent procedure to follow, with adjustment to idiolects or area dialects that are recognized as correct.

The minor pattern *ui* for /ue/, not included in the patterns to be taught, appears in *suit* and *pursuit,* but the pronunciation of *ui* in these words may also be /ထ/ to rhyme with *fruit.* It appears also in *cruiser, juice, sluice,* and *nuisance.* All usages can be treated as /ue/ or /ထ/ and should be taught directly. The *ui*'s in *build, guild, guilt, biscuit,* and *guitar* are, of course, exceptions to the use of *ui* for /ue/ or /ထ/. Here, as indicated earlier under *i,* the sound is /i/. A contrast procedure for the *ui* words should be followed.

The Diacritic u

Although *u* in *gue* endings and in beginnings of words before *e* or *i* has been described as a diacritic having the function of separating *e* and *i* from *g* to prevent decoding *g* to /j/, the diacritic functions of *u* are not limited to this kind of situation. As has been shown in the analysis of *o,* the letter *o* represents not only its own glided and unglided sounds but also the sounds /u/, /ထ/ and /ထ/. Extending the usages of *o,* we can see that if we double the letter, then *oo* represents /ထ/ or /ထ/, reducing uncertainty about the function of *o* as in *book* or *food.* In earlier times, *u* was added to *o,* permitting us to recognize that *o* in other words also represents /œ/, /au/, /ထ/, /ထ/, and /u/. *u* after *o* therefore signals the various pronunciations that *o* can represent.

Similarly, *a* represents /au/, /ɑ/, and /u/ in addition to its usual glided and unglided sounds. The addition of *u* to *a* in *laugh, auto,* and *restaurant* duplicates these representations, but *a* plus *u* also represents /œ/ in *chauffeur* and /ou/ in two positions of the word *sauerkraut.*

Since there is no consistency to the usage of *u* following *o* or *a,* after *e* or *ie* as in *feud* and *lieutenant,* or in combination with *ea* *(beau), i (fruit, build)* and *y (buy),* no attempt to show the diacritic function of *u* seems warranted, beyond the most frequent usages of /u/ and /ue/ and after *g* before *e* and *i.*

REFERENCES

Bailey, Mildred H. "The Utility of Phonic Generalizations in Grades One Through Six." *The Reading Teacher* 20 (1967): 413 – 418.

Burmeister, Lou E. "Usefulness of Phonic Generalizations." *The Reading Teacher* 21 (1968): 349 – 360.

––––––. "Vowel Pairs." *The Reading Teacher* 21 (1968a): 445 – 452.

Clymer, Theodore L. "The Utility of Phonic Generalizations in the Primary Grades." *The Reading Teacher* 16 (1963): 252 – 258.

Dewey, Godfrey. *Relative Frequency of English Spellings.* New York: Columbia University, Teachers College Press, 1970.

Emans, Robert. "The Usefulness of Phonic Generalizations Above the Primary Grades." *The Reading Teacher* 20 (1967): 419 – 425.

Groff, Patrick. "Dictionary Syllabication – How Useful?" *The Education Digest* 47 (May 1972): 49 – 51.

Hanna, Paul R., et al. *Phoneme-Grapheme Correspondences as Cues to Spelling Improvement.* Washington, D.C.: U.S. Office of Education, Bureau of Research, 1966.

Mazurkiewicz, Albert J. "The Diacritic *e.*" *Reading World* 14 (October 1974): 9 – 21.

Rinsland, Henry D. *A Basic Vocabulary of Elementary School Children.* New York: Macmillan, 1945.

Ruddell, Robert B. *Reading-Language Instruction: Innovative Practices.* Englewood Cliffs, N.J.: Prentice-Hall, 1974.

Soffietti, James. "Why Children Fail to Read: A Linguistic Analysis." In *New Perspectives in Reading Instruction,* edited by A. J. Mazurkiewicz. New York: Pitman, 1968.

Venezky, Richard. "English Orthography: Its Graphical Structure and Its Relation to Sound." *Reading Research Quarterly* 2 (1967): 75 – 106.

5
Approaches to Instruction

Learning the symbol-sound, grapheme-phoneme, combinations of English is dependent on the ability to discriminate the phonemes of English, to discriminate the graphemes used to represent these speech-sounds, and to make or learn associations between symbol and sound. Auditory and visual discrimination skills have only low to moderate correlations with reading achievement, but a child's ability to identify the distinctive features of letters is most important, and only rarely do children have to be taught the phonemes of their native language. Reactive inhibition, present in all learning, may interfere with associative learning ability, of high importance to the task of learning to decode. Spaced repetition and practice over a period of time to develop automatic responses are crucial in overcoming reactive inhibition and in developing decoding skill toward the end of using minimum cues in reading.

It is possible to decode the sixty-seven consonant graphemes to the twenty-four consonant phonemes they represent by using simple association (*b* as /b/, *bb* as /b/) and the generalizations presented in Chapter 4. The thirty-five graphemes representing the vowel phonemes can be decoded with at least 94 percent accuracy by using association procedures, when each vowel letter is identified as representing up to five vowel phonemes, and the generalizations. The remainder of the phoneme-grapheme correspondences must be learned as part of an ongoing sight vocabulary, with the aid of a dictionary. Although there are many graphemes and generalizations to be learned, you and countless other readers have accomplished this task on the road to effective reading. Most of the grapheme-phoneme associations and rules can be learned in a concentrated period of a year, and the remainder are learned over a lifetime of reading, classroom instruction, dictionary use, and speaking with others.

Rule learning, whether as simple as *b* as /b/, *f* as /f/, and *c* as /k/ or /s/ at other times, is a necessary ingredient for effective decoding. Rules, used haltingly at first, must later become automatic, and, finally, forgotten so as to prevent their interfering in the process of skillful decoding. This process uses minimum cues of letter or word features, context, and language structure to achieve rapid comprehension. Although rules have been shown to be valuable as a means of grouping information applicable to a number of graphemes, controversy as to their usage exists.

RESEARCH BASES FOR APPROACHES TO INSTRUCTION

A study by Mazurkiewicz (1975b) on the application of terms and generalizations in phonics by college professors indicated that some 69 percent teach at least ten phonic generalizations to teachers-in-training for use in word-recognition programs. Most educators do favor teaching some phonic generalizations, but research since at least 1950 has raised serious doubt about the validity of the generalizations commonly included in courses, texts, and teaching materials. The value of at least some of the findings of this research is questionable, however, because of modifications of accepted pronunciations in dictionaries, and because there is no consistency in the types of material from which sample words were taken, in the methods of selecting words from similar materials, or in authors' definitions of such terms as *short* or *long vowel sounds*. Despite these shortcomings, this research reveals the inadequacies of three of the most widely used vowel generalizations and demonstrates fairly consistently the inadequacies of a host of others. We will now look at the key studies that examined the generalizations.

Elsie Black (1950) studied 1,996 words identified by E. A. Betts as contained in certain basal readers designed for use in the primary grades to determine the incidence of certain consonant letters, blends, digraphs, and trigraphs according to their initial and final syllabic position. She found that 68 percent of all consonant usages were single consonants, while two-letter blends represented 15 percent of the total. In addition, there were 130 syllabic consonants and 16 syllabic blends. Oaks (1952) examined vowel and vowel combinations that appeared in this same vocabulary and found 103 different single-vowel correspondences, 53 vowel-digraph, and 5 diphthong usages. She also identified 8 generalizations that appeared to operate in the pronunciation of the vowel graphemes. Millard Black (1950) sought to determine the incidence of five word endings *(s, ing, ed, er,* and *est)* at each reader level in the primary grades and found that the morpheme *s* accounted for more than half the total studied. Each used Webster's *New International Dictionary* (1936) to establish pronunciations of words.

Fry's (1964) frequency count of words to which generalizations were applicable was based on his 300 "instant words," his terminology for sight words. Fry compared his findings with those of Cordts (1925), Moore (1951), Kottmeyer (1954), and Sister Mary Carlo Black (1961) and examined phonic rules formulated from his own experiences in a reading clinic. The pronunciation system that he used was taken from Moore, which in turn was based on the work of Bloomfield. His rules, however, differed from their system in several ways, most notably when he stated that *y* at the end of a word containing another vowel represents a long *e* sound. This was in direct opposition to the short *i* sound given for this position by most dictionaries until the early 1960s.

Clymer (1963: p. 253) describes such differences when he notes: "The usefulness of certain generalizations depends upon regional pronunciations. While following Webster's markings [Webster's *New Collegiate Dictionary,* 1959], generalization 34 [having to do with the /ɛɛ/ sound of *y* and *ey* at the end of words] is rejected. Midwesterners' pronunciation makes this generalization rather useful, although we reject it because we used Webster as the authority."

In pronunciations in the eastern United States (and apparently in the western, since Fry was writing in California at the time), the final sound in such words as *funny* or *baby* is identified as a glided or "long" *e,* and Webster's *Third New International Dictionary* (1963) identifies the sound as long *e* rather than the short *i.* In

Chapter 1, the *e* in unaccented syllables is identified as schwi. Fry concluded that a variety of generalizations could be structured that would be "useful." Among them were: vowels in open syllables are usually long; and the *e* at the end of words is usually silent and makes the preceding vowel long.

Clymer (1963) examined the utility of 45 phonic generalizations found among 121 in 4 "widely used" basal series at grades one through three. He combined the vocabularies from the four series with the words from the Gates *Reading Vocabulary for the Primary Grades* to determine the percent of utility of the selected generalizations. He used Webster's *New Collegiate Dictionary* as his pronunciation authority.

Bailey (1967) and Emans (1967) extended Clymer's research by computing the utility of phonic generalizations for a wider sample of words. They both studied the same 45 generalizations as did Clymer, but Bailey used the vocabularies from 8 basal series grades one through six excluding words that did not appear in two or more series, as well as place names, proper names, and foreign words. Her composite list had 5,773 words.

Emans (1967) focused on words beyond the primary level. He selected a random sample of 10 percent (1,994) of the words beyond the grade-four level in the *Teacher's Word Book of 30,000 Words* (Thorndike and Lorge, 1944).

Burmeister (1968) used a 14-level stratified random sample of the *Teacher's Word Book of 30,000 Words* to obtain an even spread of easy and difficult words to examine the validity levels of selected phonic and structural analysis generalizations. "These generalizations were selected by the author because they are commonly found in reading materials and/or have been found by her, in her teaching experience, to be particularly useful to high school students" (1968:100). She used the *American College Dictionary* (1961) as her source for pronunciation.

The results of the Clymer, Bailey, and Emans studies have been referred to in Chapter 3. Table 15 presents their results as they apply to vowels. Table 15 shows the questionable value of rules 1 and 4, two of the rules used most widely in instructing children when using the 1961 edition of Webster's *New Collegiate Dictionary.*

Although only a limited number of the 45 rules were shown to be valuable, through restructuring, 18 of the 45 generalizations could be useful, and 13 of those applied to vowels. Unfortunately, the most frequently used rules, the "final *e*" and "two vowels go

TABLE 15. The Utility of Vowel Generalizations

Generalization	Percentage of Utility		
	Clymer	*Bailey*	*Emans*
1. When there are two vowels side by side, the long sound of the first one is heard and the second is usually silent.	45%	34%	18%
2. When a vowel is in the middle of a one-syllable word, the vowel			
is short.	62	71	73
is the middle letter.	69	78	81
is one of the middle two letters in a word of four letters.	59	68	71
is one vowel within a word of more than four letters.	46	62	42
3. If the only vowel letter is at the end of a word, the letter usually stands for a long sound.	74	76	33
4. When there are two vowels, one of which is final *e*, the first vowel is long and the *e* is silent.	63	57	63
5. The *r* gives the preceding vowel a sound that is neither long nor short.	78*	86	82*
6. The first vowel is usually long and the second silent in the digraphs *ai, ea, oa,* and *ui.*	66	60	58
ai	64	72	83
ea	66	55	62
oa	97	95	86
ui	6	10	0
7. In the phonogram *ie*, the *i* is silent and the *e* has a long sound.	17	31	23
8. Words having double *e* usually have the long *e* sound.	98*	87	100*
9. When words end with silent *e*, the preceding *a* or *i* is long.	60	50	48
10. In *ay*, the *y* is silent and gives *a* its long sound.	78*	88	100
11. When the letter *i* is followed by the letters *gh*, the *i* usually stands for its long sound and the *gh* is silent.	71	71	100
12. When *a* follows *w* in a word, it usually has the sound *a* has in *was.*	32	22	28

TABLE 15. The Utility of Vowel Generalizations (Continued)

13. When *e* is followed by *w*, the vowel sound is the same as represented by *oo*.	35	40	14
14. The two letters *ow* make the long *o* sound.	59	55	50
15. *w* is sometimes a vowel and follows the vowel digraph rule.	40	33	31
16. When *y* is the final letter in a word, it usually has a vowel sound.	84*	89	98*
17. When *y* is used as a vowel in words, it sometimes has the sound of long *i*.	15	11	4
18. The letter *a* has the same sound (ô) when followed by *l*, *w*, and *u*.	48	34	24
19. When *a* is followed by *r* and final *e*, we expect to hear the sound heard in *care*.	90	96	100
20. One vowel letter in an accented syllable has its short sound.	61	65	64
21. When *y* or *ey* is seen in the last syllable that is not accented, the long sound of *e* is heard.	0	0	1
22. In many two- and three-syllable words, the final *e* lengthens the vowel in the last syllable.	46	46	42
23. When a word has only one vowel letter, the vowel sound is likely to be short.	57	69	70

*These generalizations were found to be "useful" according to the criteria that a generalization should aid a child to achieve the correct pronunciation 75 percent of the time and that it apply to at least twenty words.

walking" rules, were not improved. But when final *y* in *funny* was considered as a schwi or "long *e*," for example, the rule for final *y* was shown to have 92 percent utility. Later research by Burmeister (1968) showed that when a generalization is written to include both /ie/ and /ɛɛ/ sounds of the final *y* and *ey* (see the generalization on p. 87), it has 100 percent utility. When the research of Mazurkiewicz (1974, a, b, c) who used the Rinsland *Basic Vocabulary of Elementary School Children* of 14,571 words to identify 1,575 *e-*

ending words for his studies of the function of the silent *e*, and who studied the diacritic *i, u, h*, and others, is added to or used to modify the research of Clymer, Bailey, and Emans, a set of generalizations emerge, no one of which has less than 80 percent utility, and many of which have utilities of 90 to 100 percent.

Rather than using graphics research to discard rules, as some authors have suggested (Stauffer, 1969), it should be used to develop valuable rules that should be taught to children as opportunities arise.

Minimum-cue reading is developed by experience with print and, on the average, emerges as a characteristic of readers along with the end of directed instruction on grapheme-phoneme correspondence. In a regular orthography, such as Italian, or in a reformed orthography, such as i.t.a., minimum-cue-based reading first appears shortly after the child has mastered the associations of symbols with sounds — that point at which repetitive use of symbols begins to allow instantaneous recognition and at which point the child is fully utilizing his or her skill in blending a sequence of sounds to produce words. It regularly appears in a reformed orthography program at some point during the middle of the first year of school, usually in the equivalent of materials having a second-grade readability. This occurs only after repetitive use, by children of the same grapheme-phoneme correspondences in an estimated 1,100 different words in a running count of some 35,000 words in books, workbooks, duplicated materials, and classroom activities (Mazurkiewicz, 1967). The child, reading at a rate of 30 to 40 words per minute, demonstrates minimum-cue reading when he or she relies on instantaneous recognition of whole words rather than decoding character by character. When the child presumably recognizes whole words "instantly," we note that he or she may be using only initial letters as the cues to determine which word is intended; that in some words he or she sloughs off some letters as superfluous; that he or she is using the clue value of the upper half of most words and that he or she is giving scant attention to still others, since the context often permits him or her to "know" what words are intended to be in that position in a sentence.

The procedure of using fewer cues to recognize words is identical in the far more complex traditional orthography using the 112+ graphemes of traditional print. The rate of progression to minimum-cue-based reading is related to the extent new correspondences are controlled or sequenced and rules of correspondence are internalized. Barriers to progress may exist in either type of orthography when the child confronts a new correspondence.

In traditional print, it takes longer to progress to minimum-cue-based reading because of the larger number of grapheme-phoneme correspondences that must be mastered. Minimum-cue-based reading may also be present when sight vocabulary is regularly developed. It is added to as major correspondences are discovered or mastered, but it usually appears when children are in the second or third years of school and are using materials in which the new vocabulary is controlled.

Often, during the intermediate years of school, because grapheme-phoneme-correspondence instruction is abandoned, or because rules of correspondence are not fully developed or discovered by the child, ineffective decoding (reading) results. This poor skill in reading follows them to later grade levels and even to the college level.

It has been suggested that children can (and do) discover rules of correspondence unaided, that children can be led to discover them, and that they can also be taught them. Each of these three approaches to learning is embraced to varying extents by the authors of reading materials, yet research has shown that direct teaching is superior to the discovery or the modified discovery approaches not only for immediate learning but for long-term retention and use as well.

The approaches to instruction illustrated here use all three approaches but emphasize direct teaching. Discovery on the child's part is expected in his or her continued application of the correspondences and rules generated or taught. Correspondences and generalizations are shown as being taught using an analysis-by-synthesis procedure and also as being discovered with the assistance of certain clues.

AUDITORY DISCRIMINATION

Auditory discrimination refers to the child's ability to distinguish differences between significantly different phonemes and, in the absence of a hearing loss, may sometimes interfere in the child's development of decoding skill. Older materials assumed that much teacher-directed activity was necessary to develop auditory discrimination skills, and some authors believed that correlations between auditory discrimination and phonic-type instruction are high, though of less importance when predominantly look-say procedures are used. Since the child has usually mastered the phonemes of speech without directed instruction before entering school, we may ask if directed activity on discrimination between such similar phonemes as /i/ and /e/ is really necessary. Research has shown that auditory memory and auditory sequencing (or blending) play an important part in learning to read but that, apart from instruction on grapheme-phoneme correspondences, discrimination instruction is not required. Research has also shown that direct instruction on grapheme-phoneme relationships produces a high order of auditory discrimination skill.

Rather than emphasizing mastery of auditory discrimination, teachers should stress the development of sensitivity to the differences between closely similar phonemes and should focus on the child's approximation of the phoneme based on his or her speech characteristics. If one child rhymes *pin* with *ten*, and another rhymes it with *win*, it is difficult to determine whether this reflects dialect difference or whether the first child is having a harder time learning to read than the second. A teacher should accept all dialect differences as being correct speech productions and should *teach reading, not speech correction.* Correction of speech defects is the task of the speech therapist, and an emphasis on phoneme-grapheme correspondences is the function of the classroom teacher.

Having children attend to the phones as heard at the beginning, middle, and end of a series of words immediately prior to the introduction of a grapheme used to represent that phoneme is of direct value to learning to decode. Sound discrimination related to tapping, thumping, rapping, or scratching is unrelated to the task. A general procedure such as the following for the grapheme *a* for the phoneme /a/ illustrates the point:

"I'm going to say some words. Listen to the beginning sound in each word: *apple, axe, at, am, after.* Now listen for the sound in the middle of these words: *cat, hat, can, ran, tap, say.* Who can give me another word that has the same sound, the first sound in *apple* or the middle sound in *cat?*"

Allowing time for responses, perhaps supply such cues as: "It's something we put on our heads," or "Sometimes we call it a hat but other times we call it a _____." The introduction of the grapheme *a* follows, using a key word such as *apple* to illustrate it.

"This is the symbol, /a/, which we use to represent (stand for) the first sound in *apple* or the middle sound in *cat.*" The teacher writes the character on the board, points it out on a key-word card, in additional words, has children identify it in a series of words, teaches its formation while referring to it as "the /a/, as in *apple*," has children trace it in the air, traces the model on the chalkboard, writes the symbol, underlines the symbol in printed words, and uses some further, similar procedures.

VISUAL DISCRIMINATION

In the procedure described above, auditory-visual discrimination and association of the grapheme with its phoneme flowed together so that no one activity was isolated. But visual discrimination was required only when the child was asked to find, isolate, and mark in some fashion the grapheme used to represent the sound in the context of other graphemes. *Visual discrimination is the ability to differentiate between visual symbols,* to know, for example, that *a* is the letter *a* and not *o* or *e*, and so on.

Muehl and King (1967), reporting on a review of the research in visual discrimination, point out that

1. Training in class should be with word and letter stimuli since nonverbal stimuli (pictures, geometric forms, etc.) do not transfer to word discrimination.
2. Letter discrimination and naming letters appears to be useful.
3. Simultaneous matching of like symbols has value.
4. A three-way association of sound, meaning, and visual discrimination should be emphasized.
5. Discrimination of new words should be taught prior to reading a selection.

However, Samuels (1972), who taught one group of first-graders the names of letters, compared these children with a second group who received no such training. He tested both groups using a task of learning to say words constructed out of these letters and found that there was no significant difference between the two groups. Although Samuels repeated the experiment twice with different groups of children, he always obtained the same results. The inference that letter names are of value in communicating about alphabetic symbols but of no special value in learning to decode written language is inescapable.

Marchbanks and Levin (1965) in their research for *Project Literacy*, working with kindergarten and first-grade children found that children used first, final, and middle letters of words as well as word configuration as cues to word-identification. Additionally, they reported that the sequence of first, final, and middle letters and configuration was also the priority of importance in word-identification. The inference, as shown by Williams, Blumber, and Williams (1970) in a similar study, was that beginning readers show a strong tendency to match on the bases of individual letters rather than on word shapes. Schonell (1948) reported evidence of a similar sort much earlier, indicating that children depend upon particular details for successful recognition. Gibson (1965), as a result of her work with Levin and others, suggested that good readers are good readers because they attend and respond to the distinctive features of written symbols. Since her results demonstrated that even kindergarten children showed no greater tendency than older children to use word shape as the most important cue for word-recognition, a deemphasis on configurational and whole word (the Gestalt) approaches to instruction is suggested. This should not be surprising since, according to Piagetian decentration theory, the child is usually incapable of using field or ground characteristics (that which would give rise to configuration) until much later.

Additional studies, such as those of Pick (1965) and Lott (1969), indicate that a child who uses grapheme cues in word-recognition can transfer these cues to new words, and that grapheme recognition is not a result of maturation but must be taught.

Samuels (1972), in a further study, demonstrated that the child's knowledge of letter names is of little importance, whereas his or her recognition of the sounds those letter names contain and which are associated with the letters is of first importance in producing a correlation with reading achievement. Samuels and Williams (1973) in an AERA Conference also alluded to additional research that suggested that a knowledge of letter names may even interfere with learning to read. Although this may be true, children often know the names of letters before entering school, and such interference in learning to read is of minor importance. However, all this points out that the critical skill in beginning reading is not a knowledge of letter names but rather *the ability to recognize and discriminate graphemes.*

DISTINCTIVE FEATURES

The research of both Gibson (1970) and Anderson and Samuels (1970) points out that the child should be taught to distinguish between printed symbols using the distinctive features of letters. *Distinctive features* refers to the fact that every letter, whether manuscript or cursive, differs from every other letter in one or more ways. These differences are distinctive features. Although Gibson's earlier research (Gibson et al., 1963) suggests that it is unnecessary to point out all the features of a letter but important to point out the key features or relevant distinguishing characteristics of a letter, the procedures usually used in the classroom to teach the child to write letters include all the relevant features. The child may learn more than is necessary for decoding purposes but, at the same time, obtain information that can be called on, independently, to distinguish between letters. Gibson rightly points out that the distinguishing feature of the letters *n* and *h* is the vertical line in the top half of *h*, and that the similarities of the letters are not useful in discriminating between the two symbols.

Distinctive features of letters have been identified not only by Gibson et al. (1963) but also by Pick (1965) and others as including such characteristics as orientation on the page, open-closed, line-curve, diagonality, and vertical-horizontal line.

1. *Orientation on the page.* Such confusible letters as *b-d, p-q,* and *u-n* (as well as *M-W* and *N-Z* in the upper case) differ primarily by their orientation on the page since no distinctive features such as the tail on the *d* in the i.t.a. symbol system are provided for these letters in traditional orthography. Verbal mediation, that is, the use of a verbal description to point out that the *n* contains an arch and the *u* a hook, that *n* suggests the roundness of the object named in the key word *nest*, and so on, must be used in addition to direction-ality in formation (left-right, top-bottom) to prevent errors in discrimination.

2. *Open-closed.* The pairs *c-o* and *C-O* are discriminated primarily by one being a complete circle (closed) and the other an incomplete circle (open).

3. *Line-curve.* Since writing is made up of lines, circles, or some part of a circle (curve), these basic features of writing distinguish between upper-case *C, D, G, P* and *R* in a gross way. *C* and *G*, for example, are distinguished from *D, P,* and *R* in that the first group is round and the second group is part round. The absence of a curved line distinguishes *E, F, M, N,* and *W* from *C, G, D, P,* and *R*. The confusible pair *u-v* is basically distinguished using line-curve features.

4. *Diagonality.* Diagonal lines are also distinctive features that can be taught to children to distinguish between *M* and *N* and, with the addition of orientation on the page, *W*. This set can be distinguished from others such as *E* or *F* using diagonality. The confusible pair *P-R* relies to a large extent on the child's distinguishing the diagonal in *R*.

5. *Vertical-horizontal lines.* Such letter pairs as *I-L* and *E-F* as well as the *n-h* illustrate the concept of this distinctive feature.

Following the suggestions of research by Pick (1965), Lott (1969), and Gibson (1970), letters that are often confused with each other should be presented concurrently. Although in the sequence suggested below, a mix of vowels and consonants separates *b* from *d* by some interval of time, the letter *d* might also be presented at the same time as *b* to emphasize grapheme discrimination. The pairs *m-u, p-q,* and *v-u* can also be presented together to help the pupil focus on the distinctive feature distinguishing between them.

The example of a set of teacher statements and procedures for instruction, as shown on p. 128, uses several words having one letter in common. When the pupil is asked to find the letter that is in all the words, he or she begins to develop a learning set to search for and discriminate graphemes in words. This procedure is frequently used in most reading materials, yet confirmation that this approach — searching for graphemes — was most useful was delayed until quite recently (Gibson, 1970) when the approach was shown to encourage transfer of grapheme recognition from target words to new words.

The technique of asking pupils to locate graphemes in various positions in words also helps them to differentiate and recognize words since it requires them to make some kind of analysis of the features of the graphemes. Since beginning readers use initial, medial, and final letters as cues in word-recognition, teaching the pupil to search for and identify the graphemes in these positions will be of further aid in promoting analysis of features. Since this kind of analysis does not usually occur spontaneously, directed instruction is necessary.

REACTIVE INHIBITION IN LEARNING

Psychologists use the terms *retroactive, proactive,* and *reactive inhibition* in learning, but such terminology is often confusing to lay persons. *Retro* and *pro* indicate the directions of learning inhibition; *reactive* sums up the whole process since it includes both directions. Reactive inhibition in learning refers to the partial or complete blocking out of old memories by new learning, or to the interference by something learned in the past with the ability to remember something new. When applied to decoding, it simply means that when a child is introduced to a second symbol to associate with a sound already known to be represented by a symbol, the second symbol interferes with retention of the first symbol and the first symbol interferes with learning the second. Once the child knows, for example, that the symbol A represents the phoneme /æ/, that child may become confused when he or she is introduced to *a* as representing the same phoneme.

The child soon learns that the letter *a* cannot be depended on: it represents the phoneme /æ/ in *lady* or *baby* but never in *many.* At this point, reactive inhibition operates to deny easy retention and learning. Next, the child must learn that sometimes *a* by itself represents /æ/, but at other times *a* in combination with some other letter represents /æ/. For instance,

> *ai* in *paid* or *laid* but not in *said*
> *ay* in *day* or *play* but not in *says*
> *a-e* in *tame* or *communicate* but not in *delicate*

Reactive inhibition operates here.

Later *a* is abandoned altogether, and the child is instructed that the phoneme /æ/ is represented by other symbols:

> *ey* in *they* but not in *key*
> *eigh* in *eight* but not in *height*
> *ea* in *great* but not in *head, hear,* or *bead*

In this case, reactive inhibition operates, interfering with older memories (retroactively) and new learnings (proactively).

The teacher has several tasks: to rehearse and exercise previous learnings when a new learning is introduced; to space introduction of the variety of graphemes used to represent particular phonemes; to use comparison and contrast to show which words use a given grapheme in a set of symbols (words). Since instructional materials differ markedly, it is recommended that the teacher use only lower-case symbols in beginning reading instruction. Upper-case letters can be suggested by using larger forms of the lower-case letters. Instructional procedure should emphasize the recording of children's experiences as expressed in their language, and such language-experience records in initial reading, with books using upper- and lower-case forms delayed until mastery of the lower-case forms is complete.

INSTRUCTIONAL SEQUENCES

If we were to base an instructional sequence on research on the relative frequency of letters in English print, the first letter to be taught would be *e*. Cryptographers use the letter *e* to represent a variety of sounds and automatically substitute it for whatever letter or symbol is most frequent in a coded message. In fact, the pattern "etaoin shrdlu" closely approximates the frequency of letters used in adult reading materials. The complete sequence is as follows: *e, t, a, o, i, n, s, r, h, l, d, u, c, f, m, w, y, g, p, v, k, x, j, q, z* (Dewey, 1923). Since *e* most frequently represents the unglided /e/ and next most frequently represents the unglided /u/ in unstressed positions, little opportunity for the development of meaningful recognition vocabulary is available when the first six letters are combined to form words. True, there are the words *at, on, in,* and *it* as initial possibilities, but if *e* and *t* are introduced first, no meaningful words except *tee* are possible.

Using the relative frequency of English speech-sounds in contexts used by adults gives us the order /i/, /n/, /t/, /r/, /s/, /d/, /u/, /l/, /a/, and so on (Dewey, 1923). But in the relatively limited vocabulary of children and in materials written for children, a different order is found.

The recommended procedure is to use a frequency of sound order for utility in writing and, simultaneously, reading. Initially, it is closer to the sequence *e, t, a, o, i, n* but follows the sound occurrences more closely in the latter half of the sequence reported by

Dewey based on adult materials. The recommended procedure is to teach both vowels and consonants in an interspersed order to develop a reading-writing vocabulary as quickly as possible. Although glided vowels are sometimes taught before the unglided in some phonic programs, the unglided vowel sounds are the most frequent. /æ/ and /ɛɛ/ appear as the sixteenth and nineteenth in frequency in adult materials and the eighteenth and nineteenth in children's materials, but the unglided vowels appear earlier and are the more frequent in either type of research.

No sequence of vowel-consonant phonemes and generalizations exists apart from the vocabulary sequence selected by the author or authors for a given set of materials or stories. Sequences suggesting that at a particular grade level children should have learned so many consonants, vowels, digraphs, generalizations, and so on reflect some materials of the 1940s but are irrelevant to current materials. Such sequences should never have been accepted as the only way to proceed or presumed to limit or direct what should be taught or in what order.

A diagnostic instructional approach established for a beginning program might utilize the graphemes *a, n, nn, t, e,* and *b,* during the first week of instruction. By the end of the first day of instruction, the beginning of the development of set for diversity would be established and the first part of the first generalization introduced: *vowels followed by one or two consonants are usually unglided.* Since the association of the letter *a* with /a/ and *e* with /e/ can be made without the need to teach the generalization, some might question whether teaching the generalization should be done at this time. But the opportunity is available to begin recognition of the generalization, and the practice of delaying grapheme-phoneme associations until a set number of words has been learned as sight words has no empirical basis. Associations of symbol with sound should be started as early as the first day of instruction, with sight-word development begun and continued as the opportunity arises.

For example, the word *the,* or, as some writers identify it, the "word sign" *the,* can be introduced during the first week of instruction with any of the nouns developed from phonic teaching, *the bat, the net, the tent, the ant,* and continued with additional words in the second week to develop a further level of skill in blending words to reflect speech melody (as indicated by stress): *the best, the best nest, the ant sat, the ant bit, the ant ran, Nan ran, an ant ran.*

The use of language-experience records from the first day of instruction not only provides the opportunity to develop a story line for use in developing initial "reading" activities but also provides the basis for pointing out that "what can be said, can be written down; and what can be written down can be read." Such records also provide printed material to use in identifying graphemes in the context of different words. This continues the practice of developing a learning set to search for and discriminate graphemes in words as well as to locate graphemes in various positions.

The introduction of the grapheme *a* in initial activities can be used to establish the learning set or mind set that graphemes don't always represent the same sound. Described as establishing a set for diversity, the procedure is necessary since children who are taught that one symbol represents one sound have difficulty in making the transition to reading words where the same symbol represents different sounds (Levin, 1963). In traditional orthography one grapheme can be used to represent at least six different sounds. The grapheme *a* as in *a tent* does not represent /a/ as in *at* or /æ/ as in *baby;* but most often, when used as a word meaning "one," has the sound value /u/ in speech. Speakers rarely say /æ/ *book*, /æ/ *horse*, /æ/ *dog*, /æ/ *pencil*, unless there is some reason to stress the word. In normal speech the sound /u/ occurs since it's an unstressed part of the phrase.

The activities of the first day of instruction, at which time *a*, *n*, and *t* have been introduced and utilized in various ways, should culminate in some demonstration that the motivation children most often have for coming to school — namely, to learn to read and write — has been met in some small fashion. The dictation of the phrase "a tan ant," for example, to be written by pupils on their drawings of an ant, provides the most natural opportunity to point out that "When I said 'a tan ant,' you couldn't write the first word because I didn't say /a/. /a/ when used as a word is usually pronounced /u/. Listen to these words: *a book, a dog, a pencil, a house.*

"Whenever you see the letter /a/ as in *apple* by itself, it's used as a word to mean 'one,' and you should think and say /u/ since that's the way we normally say it. Now write: *a tan ant.*" Thus the third most frequent sound represented by *a* can be introduced and a *set* to expect that symbols can represent more than one sound begun.

Since other words of interest to pupils, related to continuous needs or language-experience records, might also be taught as sight words and used similarly, delay in instruction in the grapheme-phoneme correspondences is not warranted. Indeed, research and practice in strong decoding-emphasis programs suggest the opposite.

A SEQUENCE OF GRAPHEME-PHONEME CORRESPONDENCES

The elaborated sequence presented in Table 16 pulls together information from Chapters 3 and 4. The compilation should not be taken to mean that all the consonant or vowel graphemes following a phoneme are to be taught at the time a phoneme with its most frequent representations are taught. Rather, it must be taken to indicate that as words can be encoded with graphemes, as words in experience stories or printed materials appear that contain the patterns, then the relevant patterns and generalizations can be taught. Since the word *rabbit,* for example, could be encoded by the introduction of the graphemes related to the seventh phoneme, the generalization that the two letters *bb* represent one sound would be relevant to call to the attention of pupils. This would join this rule for *bb* with *nn,* which could have been illustrated as early as the first day of instruction using the name *Ann.* However, *tt* might be delayed until much later, and by then the generalization for two consonants representing one sound might need little attention.

TABLE 16. Grapheme-Phoneme Correspondences

Phoneme	Key Word	Graphemes	Applicable Notes
/a/	apple	a[1, 2]	*laugh* is taught as sight word and thus includes *augh*
/n/	nest	n, nn,[1] kn, gn	
/t/	table	t, tt,[1] ed	
/e/	Eskimo	e,[1] ea, e-e	
/b/	bell	b, bb[1]	
/s/	Santa	s, c,[2] ss[1]	
/r/	rabbit	r, rr,[1] wr	
/i/	Indian	i,[1] y,[1] a-e, iu	*a-e* represents /e/ in unstressed syllables

TABLE 16.   Grapheme-Phoneme Correspondences (Continued)

Phoneme	Key Word	Graphemes	Applicable Notes
/d/	dog	d, dd,[1] ed	
/l/	lion	l, ll[1]	
/th/	feather	th,[9, 10]	
/œ/	boat	o,[1, 2] o-e,[4] ow, oa,[7] ou, oe[3]	
/m/	monkey	m, mm[1]	
/c/	cat	c,[2] cc[1, 3]	
/v/	valentine	v, and f in the single word *of*	
/p/	pencil	p, pp[1]	
/æ/	angel	a,[1] a-e,[4] ai,[7] ay,[7] ea	*eigh, ey,* and *aigh* are taught as grapheme bases
/ɛɛ/	eagle	e,[1, 2] y,[8] ea, ee,[3] ie,[3] e-e,[4] ey,[8] i,[1] ei	*ei* taught as a variable grapheme
/f/	fish	f, ff,[1] ph,[7] lf	*lf* may be taught as a grapheme for /f/ or that *l* is silent
/w/	wagon	w	
/u/	sun	u,[1] a, e, o, ou, i, a-e, ea	*a, e, i,* and *o* follow generalization 1, but 9 and 10 are also applicable
/ω/	boot	oo,[1, 2] u, o, ou, u-e, ew,[11] ue, o-e	generalizations 1 and 2 are applicable when *oo* is taught as one grapheme
/ur/	girl	er,[10] ir,[10] yr[10]	
/ie/	ice cream	i-e,[4] i,[1] igh, y,[8] ie,[3] y-e[4]	*igh* is taught as a grapheme base
/h/	horse	h, wh[11]	
/k/	key	k, lk, ck,[1] q	*lk* may be taught as a digraph for *k*. The *l* may also be taught as silent or *alk* taught as a grapheme base
/au/	automobile	o,[6] a,[5] au,[5] aw,[5] ough, augh	*augh* and *ough* are taught as grapheme bases

TABLE 16.   Grapheme-Phoneme Correspondences (Continued)

Phoneme	Key Word	Graphemes	Applicable Notes
/ŋ/	ring	n, ng	g can be taught as a diacritic signaling the /ŋ/ pronunciation of n
/ʃh/	shoe	sh,[7] ti,[14] ssi,[14] s,[18] si,[13, 14] sci[14]	
/ω/	book	oo,[1] u, ou, o, ue, ould	ould is taught as a grapheme base or by contrast procedures
/g/	goat	g, gg,[1] gh[8]	gg in suggest equals gj
/y/	yo-yo	y, i	
/ou/	oui	ou, ow	ou taught as one grapheme
/ch/	chair	ch[6]	
/a/	arm	a,[12] a-e, ea	
/j/	jack-o'-lantern	g,[4] j, dg	
/th/	thanksgiving	th[9]	
/wh/	whistle	wh[11]	
/ue/	United States	u,[1] u-e,[4] ew,[11] ue[3]	
/oi/	boy	oi, oy	taught as graphemes representing /oi/
/ʒ/	television	si,[13] s,[13, 18] ss, z	
/z/	zebra	z, zz[1]	

NOTE: The superscripts refer to the applicable consonant or vowel generalizations found in the text.

Reference to Chapters 3 and 4 should be made wherever consonant and vowel generalizations are not discussed directly. As suggested in those chapters and in Table 16, certain words must be taught as sight words since no generalizations are possible or the patterns exist in too few words to merit the development of a generalization. Reference to grapheme bases (a group of letters found in a series of words) indicates another alternative approach to instruction with such graphemes as *igh*, *aigh*, and *augh*. The complete listing of consonant and vowel generalizations having high utilities, 80 percent or better, are also listed below for ready reference. Chapter 4 provides further illustration of the approaches possible for vowel and grapheme instruction.

CONSONANT GENERALIZATIONS

1. Two consonants together in a word usually represent one sound.

2. *c* before *e*, *i*, and *y* usually represents the sound of *s* in *Santa*.

3. The double *c* before *e* and *i* usually represents two sounds, the /k/ in *key* and the /s/ in *Santa*.

4. *g* before *e*, *i* and *y* usually represents the sound of *j* in *giraffe*.

5. *c* and *g* followed by *e* at the end of words are usually pronounced /s/ and /j/, respectively.

6. *h* after *c* indicates that the *c* can be pronounced /ʧh/, /k/, and /sh/; try the /ʧh/ sound first. *ch* before another consonant is always pronounced /k/.

7. *sh* and *ph* always represent one sound; *sh* represents /ʃh/ and *ph*, /f/.

8. *h* after *g* indicates that *g* represents /g/ at the beginning of words and /f/ at the end of words; but *gh* is usually silent.

9. *h* after *t* indicates that *t* may be pronounced /ʧh/ or /ʧh/; try the /ʧh/ sound first at the beginning and in the middle of words, and /ʧh/ first at the end of words.

10. *e* after *th* at the end of words indicates that the *th* represents /ʧh/.

11. *h* after *w* indicates that the letters are pronounced /h w/, but that before *o*, only the *h* is usually pronounced.

12. *e* after *s* indicates that *s* may be pronounced /s/ or /z/; try the /z/ sound first.

13. *s* followed by *y*, *i*, or *u* in the middle of words may be pronounced /ʒ/ or /ʃh/; try the /ʒ/ sound first.

14. *i* following *c*, *s*, *ss*, *sc*, or *t* in the last part of words is usually silent and indicates that these graphemes usually represent the /ʃh/ sound.

15. *e* following *v* and *z* at the end of words is silent and indicates only that *v* and *z* rarely come at the end of a word.

16. *e* following *ng* at the end of a word indicates that the *n* and *g* represent their own sounds and are pronounced /n/ and /j/, respectively.

17. *e* following a consonant plus *l* at the end of a word indicates that the *l* is pronounced /ul/.

18. *e* at the end of *dure, ture, sure* and *zure* endings of words indicates that *d, t, s* and *z* are pronounced /j/, /ʧh/, /ʃh/, and /ʒ/, respectively.

VOWEL GENERALIZATIONS

•1. A single vowel followed by one or two consonants usually stands for an unglided (or short) sound, but it may also be glided (or long); try the unglided (or short) sound first.

2. If the only vowel is the end of a two- or three-letter word, the grapheme usually represents a glided (or long) sound, but *a* is pronounced /a/.

3. *e* following a vowel at the end of words indicates that the vowel usually represents a glided (or long) sound.

4. *e* following a vowel and a consonant (other than the consonants *c, g, l, ng, s, th, v, z,* and the grapheme *ur*) indicates that the vowel usually represents a glided (or long) sound.

5. *a* before *l,* and in the spellings *au* and *aw,* usually represents /a/.

6. *o* before *r* represents /au/ or /œ/; try the /au/ sound first.

7. When the graphemes *ai, ay, ee,* and *oa* are seen together in a word, the first vowel usually represents its glided (or long) sound.

8. *y* usually represents /ie/ at the end of short words, but *y* and *ey* represent /ee/ in long words.

9. Vowel letters before *m, n, l,* or *r* in the last part of words having two or more vowel sounds are usually pronounced /u/.

10. *e, i,* and *y* followed by *r* usually represent the /u/ sound.

11. After *r, l, s, ch,* and *j, ew* usually represents /oo/; after other letters, /ue/.

12. *a* before *r* usually represents /a/.

INSTRUCTIONAL ACTIVITIES

The following sequence of activities are based on the research findings indicated earlier and may be utilized at preschool, first-grade, or later remedial levels, where confusion or incomplete learning is often found. Since many children will have developed a variety of skills from such television programs as *Sesame Street* or *Electric Company* and from parental or sibling prompting or instruction, the alert teacher should not repeat instruction that has already been covered and should move on to more difficult or challenging activities. Recourse to the use of simpler activities should also be made when confusion is identified.

Matching Like Letters

Using the chalkboard, a set of four or five letters, two of which are the same, may be written down, for example, *a, e, a,* and *n.* One child might be asked to come to the board and draw a line under or around the two letters that are alike. Since the child's understanding of the meaning of *alike* might cause some initial difficulty, the teacher should remember to explain that it means "the same" or "exactly the same." It is sometimes necessary to point out that the two letters selected look exactly the same. In illustration, the teacher should continue to point out that the two *a*'s are the same since they each have an arch, a line, a circle, and a hook. Separating the features of the letter *a* into its components is a useful procedure to call attention to its distinctive features as well as to illustrate how that letter can be written. Naming the parts of letters provides the information necessary for the child to distinguish between letters at later points.

These procedures can be used with upper-case versions of the same letters with the same level of difficulty in matching. A more difficult matching task to ask the child would be to select from a pile the letters that match a letter on the board. An even more difficult task is to display a letter, next remove or cover it, and then have pupils locate the same letter from memory among several others listed on the board. Exercises of this sort might be developed between seated pairs of pupils using small letter cards and individual pocket charts. Duplicated materials for whole class activity can be used to extend skills of matching like letters.

Although research suggests that letter names should not be used to refer to the letters at this point, many children enter school knowing some or all of the letter names and often can also match the letter with its name. Letter naming cannot be avoided totally since pupils will refer to a letter as an /æ/, and so on. However, the teacher should not use letter names at this point and might instead use the more frequent sounds the letters represent—the /a/ as in *apple,* the /n/ as in *nest*—or point out that letters have names and stand for sounds: "In talking about letters we can use their names but right now we don't need to use the letter names."

Matching Upper-case and Lower-case Pairs

When the pupil is required to match upper-case and lower-case pairs, letter names or the sounds the symbols represent must, however, come into use. There is no physical or graphic match between such letter pairs as *A*-a, *E*-e, and *R*-r, but there is an almost one-to-one match between the upper- and lower-case letter pairs *C*-c, *O*-o, *S*-s, *W*-w, *X*-x, and *Z*-z, which differ only in size. Matching activities such as those described above can be used for the second group without recourse to letter names or sounds, and thus activities should be structured with this group first. Beginners are less confused and the concept of capital letters more easily developed when the terms *large* and *small* rather than *upper-case, lower-case,* and *capital letters* are used in initial activities.

Language-experience records can be written using a larger form of the lower-case letter to represent the capital letter for first letters of sentences, names, and the like, thus avoiding the use of different letter forms in initial activities. When the upper-case forms are introduced, an association between sound or name and symbol is needed so that the child can see that two (or more) different letters represent the same sound or have the same name. No reactive inhibition operates in the use of a larger form of the same letter to represent the capital-letter concept, since the letter features are the same, differing only in size. But the introduction of a second form for the same letter name or sound is an associative learning activity and reactive inhibition does operate.

Simple matching activities using only upper-case forms would follow the procedures outlined above. Matching upper- and lower-case forms in the absence of letter names or sounds might be developed using an alphabet chart, where both upper- and lower-case forms are illustrated. The teacher could point out: "Some letters look alike whether they are large or small, but others are entirely different. Each letter of the alphabet has two basic forms, and both stand for the same sound or have the same letter name."

Pupils can be asked to select upper- or lower-case letters from a pile and match them with the same and then equivalent forms on the chart. The teacher should point out that the letters do not *look* alike but are similar in that they represent the same sound or have the same letter name. The use of framing techniques—where the teacher or child places his or her hands on either side of the letter to isolate it from the context of other letters in response to the direction to find the letter that is like a given letter—is a variation often found useful.

Discriminating Unlike Letters

Earlier activity suggested the identification of the features of individual letters for later use in discriminating between different letters. This was based on evidence which showed that discrimination rests on the ability to note distinctive features that differentiate between letters. Discrimination activities at this time should focus on these distinctive features between letters rather than on similarities between them. Unlike reformed orthographies, where the letter *d* is differentiated from the letter *b* by the addition of a tail, and where many symbols are wholly different from each other, traditionally printed letters require that such features as orientation on the page, open-closed and line-curve characteristics, diagonality, and vertical-horizontal lines be continuously used to distinguish between them.

Teaching procedures should first emphasize letters that are wholly unlike each other or that cannot be easily confused. In either case, the pupil should be asked to tell how the letters differ or to identify the feature(s) that differentiate the forms. The pupil should not be asked to identify *all* the features of each letter pair; rather, the emphasis should be on the distinctive features that differentiate the members of the pair. Since many letters are not easily confused, this activity is not required on all fifty-two letter forms. A particular letter should ordinarily be presented first with a highly contrastive letter, one with a very different shape, and later with a symbol with which it is often confused. The letters *d* and *b* are highly confusible as are *n* and *u*, *m* and *w*, and *p* and *q*. Thus, first present *d* with *n*, *p* with *u*, and *b* with *m*, and then *d* with *b*, *n* with *u*, and so on, as illustrated below.

1. Write the highly contrastive pair of letters *d* and *n* in manuscript form on the chalkboard. Then ask, "Are these letters the same or different? Who can tell me how they are different?" The teacher might expect answers such as, "one has a circle and a line, and the other has two lines and an arch," but should not demand or look for precise language descriptions.
2. Write the letters *d* and *o* (a less contrastive, somewhat confusible pair) on the chalkboard and follow the same procedure as above.
3. Write the letters *d* and *b* (a highly confusible pair) and ask, "Are these letters the same or different? If different, what makes

them different?" Expected responses would relate to orientation on the board; for instance, "The circle is on the left for the first letter and on the right for the second."

4. Continue with other contrastive and confusible pairs such as *q* and *u* or move to the activities suggested in steps 6 and 7. Return later to steps 4 and 5.

5. Write *d* and *q* on the board. These are highly confusible based on the identical features they share, but they differ in terms of the direction of the vertical line (or "extension," as named by Gibson). Ask again: "Are these letters the same or different? What makes them different?"

6. Continue with *p-b*, *g-p*, and so on to help children note the recurring features that discriminate between letters.

7. Have children locate a particular letter among several confusible letters in a row, using either a pocket chart or duplicated materials. Give the direction: "Find this letter in the rows of letters." This requires that the teacher either display a letter card or write the letter on the board. Duplicated materials might include the direction: "Find another letter in each row that is like the first letter."

Examples of confusible letter forms for use in steps 3, 5, and 6 include:

b-p, *d-g*, *q-d*, which differ in the direction of the extension
b-d, *q-p*, *g-p*, which differ in left-right orientation
m-w, *n-u*, *M-W*, which differ in top-bottom orientation
u-v, *U-V*, which differ in line-curve features

Note that *n-u* can also be differentiated in such terms as the *n* having an arch or part of a circle at the top, while the *u* has a part of a circle (a hook) at the bottom, and that in some printed materials *m* differs markedly from *w* in that *m* contains curves but *w* contains lines only. The list of confusible pairs that follows can be used in the generalized procedures described above for daily activity in initial reading activities.

Lower-Case Confusible Pairs	Upper-Case Confusible Pairs
a-d	C-G
a-o	D-O
b-d	E-F

b-h	I-J
b-p	I-L
b-q	K-X
c-e	L-T
c-o	M-W
d-q	O-Q
d-g	P-R
d-p	U-V
f-t	V-Y
g-p	
g-q	
h-n	
i-j	
m-n	
m-w	
n-u	
p-q	
u-v	
v-w	
v-y	

Locating Letters in Words

A natural follow-up to step 7 is to locate, frame, underline, or circle particular letters in a list of words or in an experience story. Several additional considerations must be taken into account here, and thus locating letters in words is separated from the sequence described above. Reading requires the ability to discriminate and identify letters in the context of a word, and in such a context the surrounding print on the page may confuse the pupil. This print is essentially distracting "noise" that the pupil must visually "tune out" in order to attend to the features of particular words or letters.

Pronunciation of the words in a list of words or an experience story is ordinarily avoided since it distracts from the task of recognizing particular graphemes. Lists of words should be provided so that pupils can locate particular letters in initial, medial and final positions. Furthermore, they should work on, for instance, the *b* in *ban*, *tab*, or *cabin* before they are asked to locate the letter *b* in *band*, *bad*, *bid*, or *body*, which contain confusible letters.

When the words on a list contain only one letter in common and the child is asked to "find the letter that is the same in all the words," a more difficult task is involved. Specific procedures follow:

1. List on the board several words that begin with the same letter. Ask pupils to come to the board and underline the letter in the words.
2. List words that end with the same letter; repeat the procedure.
3. List words that contain the same letter in a medial position; repeat the procedure.
4. Have pupils find that letter in experience-story materials.
5. List words containing one letter in common in various positions and ask children to "find the letter that is the same in all the words."
6. List words that contain both the particular letter and a confusible letter and repeat the procedure.

Grapheme-Phoneme Correspondence

Although Chall (1967) concluded that a focus on decoding strategy rather than on meaning produced better achievement, that argument still exists. It has also been difficult to lay to rest the fiction that a discovery approach is better than a didactic approach, even though research and widescale practical experience clearly demonstrates that direct instruction is superior to deductive-discovery approaches to learning. But, as has been demonstrated by a variety of studies, learning to read relates directly to learning the grapheme-phoneme correspondences of the language. Bishop (1964), for example, working with college sophomores, trained two groups to read Arabic words; he used a whole-word method with one group and a method that emphasized grapheme-phoneme correspondences with another. When the subjects were asked to read new words, which were made by recombining the various symbols that had been presented, the group trained by emphasizing grapheme-phoneme correspondences showed significantly superior skill. Although the whole-word group showed some skill in reading the new words, this was accounted for by a small number of the whole-word subjects who had determined the grapheme-phoneme correspondences contained in the original words for themselves. In a similar experiment with six-year-olds, using English words, Jeffrey and Samuels (1967) found that transfer to decoding new words was based on the use of letter-sound correspondences alone.

Bleismer and Yarborough (1960) experimented with ten different approaches to teaching reading in the first grade, comparing meaning (whole-word) emphasis programs with decoding emphasis programs, and concluded that strong directed instruction on symbol-sound correspondences produced significantly greater reading achievement than approaches that emphasized whole words and discovery-type learning of phonics. In comparing a directed phonic-type i.t.a. program with a look-say discovery procedure that used the same materials, Tudor-Hart (1969) also found that directed phonics instruction produced superior achievement.

Discovery-type decoding instruction, though successful in the case of many pupils, apparently has not been effective in increasing reading achievement in a large number of others since, according to Piagetian theory, the average child has not yet developed sufficient cognitive skills to allow him or her to induce the grapheme-phoneme relationships. At the same time, some experts deride the direct instructional approach of teaching the pupil that the letter *b* or *d* represents the phoneme /b/ or /d/ since it is assumed that teachers are incapable of pronouncing single consonant phonemes in isolation. Discovery procedures have been suggested as a way to avoid the distortions sometimes heard when, for example, teachers attempt to isolate the speech-sound /b/ and instead produce /bu/. The experts reason that children are incapable of sounding out the word *bat* by a procedure that produces /bu-a-tu/ and of understanding that that combination of sounds represents *bat*. But surely it would be just as wrong to expect children to spell out the word *bat* using letter-name knowledge, which these experts often recommend as a first step, and to expect children to understand that /bεε-æ-tεε/ represents *bat*. In fact, the arguments for a discovery approach and for letter-name knowledge are unrelated to what children actually do when confronted with an unknown word. Observations on thousands of children taught by didactic and discovery-type procedures have shown that children do indeed sound out unknown words, most often producing vocalizations that correspond to /bu-a-tu/, whether taught by didactic or discovery-type methods and, based on their cognitive skills, pronounce the words correctly.

If the teacher instructs directly that the letter *b* as in *bell* represents the /b/ sound, and even if some distortion exists, this would provide a child with more useful information for decoding than if he or she has been instructed that the letter *b* has the name /bεε/. Both methods are, however, merely alternate ways of naming letters. If no other additional instruction is given using the context of words or units of syllable size, then neither procedure will be particularly effective in aiding the child to develop decoding skill.

Didactic instruction provides the child the information that the letter *b* represents /b/ and is always related to the /b/ sound in a key word such as *bell* to reduce or eliminate the schwa or /u/-like following sound after the phoneme /b/ and to demonstrate that sound in the natural sound context of a word. Auditory perception of the sound in various positions is followed by an examination of words such as *bat, bin, Ben, ban, tab, cab, rub, cub, cabin,* and *rabbit* to move from the isolated sound to its place in the context of words. The child is asked to tell which letter is the same at the beginning or end of such words as *ban, bat, tab,* and *cab;* is asked to listen to beginning and ending sounds in these words; and is told again that the letter represents the sound /b/ as in *bell.* Application to additional words should then follow.

In discovery-type instruction, on the other hand, the child is asked to listen for the sound that begins or ends words in a series and then to attend to and discriminate it in the medial position of words. This activity of auditory perception is also followed by the examination of a list of words. The child is asked to tell which letter is the same in each of such words as *bat, bed, ban, tab,* and *cab;* to listen to the beginning and ending sound in each of these words; to note that the sound is the same as the beginning sound in the key word *bell;* and then to apply that sound to new words listed.

This analysis shows that the only essential difference between the two generalized instructional approaches is that in the didactic approach children are told the sound that the letter *b* represents, and in the discovery-type method, they find it out for themselves. In the didactic approach, the chance for error in developing a clear-cut association of symbol with sound is reduced or eliminated since children are not only told that a given letter represents a given sound and asked to attend to that sound in the context of words, they are also provided with additional reinforcement in the form of reminders that a particular letter represents a particular sound or sounds. In the discovery approach, the chance for error in association is greater since, as research suggests, only with increased maturity are children capable of moving from the phrase to isolating a word, syllable, or speech-sound in the phrase. Therefore, they may be unable to separate a specific sound at the beginnings and ends of words let alone to isolate it in the medial position of words. Since children are supplied with no direct information, they may often simply guess at what they're supposed to glean from such activity.

A better discovery-type instructional model, which includes learning to write and utilize a letter in words, isolates a letter and supplies children with the sound the letter represents. At this point, children can make a clear-cut association of symbol with sound. Any error in association in initial activities is corrected by ensuring that the child writes the correct letter to represent the sound that begins, ends, or is contained in the medial position of words. Repetitive use fixates the correct association.

The two models, didactic and discovery, also differ in that in the didactic method the rule is stated and is followed by an illustration or examples, whereas in the discovery method, examples are provided and the child is expected to generalize or discover the rule. Logic indicates that the didactic approach is superior since it leaves nothing to chance. This approach has also been described pejoratively as a "synthetic" approach. That is, it is assumed that in the didactic approach the child simply learns that b represents /b/, e represents /e/, t represents /t/ and is then encouraged to synthesize a word, in this case, the word /bet/. It is assumed that in the discovery-type, or "analytic," approach the child does not synthesize words from his or her discoveries. In fact, the child, when asked to write words, is encoding sounds and is thus always synthesizing words. So too when he discovers the sound that letters represent and then confronts a new word, he or she goes through the procedure that s equals /s/, a equals /a/, and t equals /t/ to arrive at /sat/. But, as has been shown, the didactic approach ensures that clear-cut information for association is supplied; uses the same auditory and visual activities as found in discovery approaches; and encourages the child to decode words using the procedure that if m equals /m/ and e equals /ɛɛ/, then m-e equals /mɛɛ/, which the child is also expected to do in the discovery approach.

Linguists may argue that children do not learn to speak by first learning sounds and then putting them together to form words, but reading in the acquisition stage is decoding to speech, which the child already possesses, and requires the child to learn that given symbols or symbol combinations represent certain speech units. Thus, reading at this stage is not a procedure of learning letter-sound association to make words but one of decoding print to speech. Our concern here is not how the child learns to speak but how he or she learns to decode print to speech. Although the work of educational psychologists, psycholinguists, and communication theorists is relevant, pragmatic experience with thousands of children is even more so. The didactic, or the "teach 'em damn it, teach 'em," approach based on pragmatic experience is preferred if our concern is to eliminate or reduce the chance for error and to minimize frustration and failure for the child as he or she learns to read.

The recommended general procedure below follows the principles that children learn to associate symbols with language they already know within the context of words, and that transfer practice is always provided. Syllable-size contexts might also be used, but all illustrations provided here use words.

Regular Consonant Letters or Clusters

The use of the term "regular" at this point is made to distinguish between consonant letters and clusters, which usually represent only one sound (b-/b/) and those which represent more than one sound (s-/s/, /z/, /ʃh/, /ʒ/). The term "cluster" is used instead of the older term "blend" to more accurately identify the specific letters referred to. Since all sounds are blended to produce a word, a blend could refer to any combination of consonants or vowels and consonants: *na* as well as *an; ba* as well as *at; bl* as well as *nd;* and so on.

Starting with instruction on single-consonant letters, a letter card and/or a key-word card should be available for use and reference in the following procedure:

1. Display the letter card or picture card (often called key-word) for *n*, for example, pointing out the letter while masking the word which identifies the object pictured, and indicating to the class or group that you are "going to say some words that begin with the sound that letter represents. Listen carefully while I say them: *nest, nickel, nice, nose.*" Since this activity is initially purely auditory, the words should not be written nor the word cards displayed at this time. Next ask: "In what way do the *nest, nickel, nice, nose* words sound alike?" Confirm or provide the information that they all begin "with the same sound /n/ as in *nest.*"

2. "Now listen to the last sound in these words: *tan, man, pen, win, ten.* Did you hear the sound /n/ as in *nest* at the end of the words?"

3. "Now listen as I say three words. Two words will begin with the same sound. Listen carefully and tell me which words begin

like *nest* and *nose*. The words are: *never, nurse, kite.*" Repeat this exercise using other triads such as *neck, sack, needle,* or *night, knife, horse.*

4. Ask the children to supply other words that "begin or end with the sound /n/ as in *nest.*"

5. Continue the same type of activity as in steps 1 or 2 but use words containing *n* in a medial position, such as *tent, ant,* and *band.*

6. Use pairs of words such as *run-rub, ten-hen, run-furs, pen-pick, lion-clean, can-man, sick-men,* and *nine-fine* in a game-type activity to provide practice in discrimination and to determine, for later treatment, which children are having difficulty discriminating the sound /n/ at the beginning and end of words.

7. Refer to the key-word card, display or write the word, and point out the letter *n* at the beginning of the word. Indicate that the letter represents (stands for) the sound /n/. Display three or four vocabulary cards containing words beginning with the letter *n.* Pronounce the words and emphasize that all the words begin with the same letter, *n.* Then pronounce the words again and emphasize that all the words begin with the same letter *and* with the same sound, /n/ as in *nest.*

8. Say some additional words beginning with the sound /n/, then write the words on the board to demonstrate that all the words begin with the same sound. Have children underline the first letter of these words. Ask, "Which letter stands for the sound of the /n/ in *nest*?"

9. On the board, write two words, one which begins with *n* and one of which does not, such as *nose* and *kite,* and ask children, "Which word begins with /n/ as in *nest*?"

10. Supply additional words ending in /n/ and repeat activities as noted in steps 8 and 9.

Supplementary Activities

Supply duplicated materials for children to use in underlining the letter *n* in various positions. Have children identify the "/n/ as in *nest*" in experience stories or other printed materials. After a set of several vowel and consonant letter associations have been made, and even as early as the first day of activity, where *a, n,* and *t* are introduced, transfer practice can be established. If the letters *a* and *n* are the only ones that have been learned, children could be encouraged to recognize *a* and *n* as the word *an* and to recognize that *n* added to *an* represents the new word *Nan.* The concept of capital letters can be introduced by using lower-case letters written one-fourth again as large, and by then pointing out that when the initial *n* in *Nan* is larger the word represents the girl's name. As suggested earlier, learning upper-case letters should be deferred till later, but the teacher may wish to teach both upper- and lower-case letters through matching in order to ensure that pupils understand that *n* and *N*, for example, represent the same sound.

With the addition of an association of /t/ with *t*, the new word *tan* can provide initial transfer practice. Later transfer practice, using such combinations as *at* and *an* learned during the initial day's activities, can be provided when other consonants, clusters, and digraphs have been learned. First write two columns of words:

at	an
fat	man
bat	ran

Next pronounce all the words and call attention to the pronunciation of the first consonant in each of the two words in each column. Add the word *mat* to the first column, encouraging children to add the next word to the same column using the first letter of the word *ran* to form *rat*, then to add the letters *f* and *b* to *an* in the second column to form *fan* and *ban*. Generalizing the symbol-sound correspondences from one column to another aids the child in developing skill in decoding.

Similar procedures can be used with consonant clusters (two- or three-letter sequences, each of which represents a distinct sound) and digraphs (two letters representing one sound) by adding *fl* or *br* to *at*; *st* or *gr* to *and*; *bl, str, tr, dr, sh* to *ip*; *ch* to *at* or *in*; and so on, to provide for generalization and transfer practice. Another exercise might encourage the use of single consonant associations such as *s* and *t, b* and *l, s* and *p* to develop words such as *stick, blend,* and *spin* by writing three columns of words such as the following:

sick	tick	stick
bend	lend	blend
sin	pin	spin

Pronounce the words in columns 1 and 2 and encourage children to try the word in column 3. Other procedures might include a three-column list of words emphasizing only *b* and *l* or *s* and *t*.

Although the teacher should avoid the distortions /nu/, /bu/, /du/, /fu/, and so on, do not indicate that *n* "says" /n/ or *d* "makes" the /d/ sound. Letters do not say or make anything; they represent or stand for sounds. *We* say or make sounds. On the other hand, children who do say /nu/, /du/, and so on, who do distort in referring to the /n/ or /d/ sounds, are not to be admonished or corrected since this stage is transitory, and the distortion merely reflects their logical understanding of how the sound is to be referred to. Constant reference to the /b/ as in *bell*, the /n/ as in *nest*, and the /t/ in *table* places the sound in a word context, assigns it its appropriate value, and helps children understand that their distortion is not the pronunciation. Reference to the sound in the following fashion, "You've been working with the /n/ sound as in *nest*," provides for a clear-cut association of symbol with sound.

The teacher must always take into account consistent variations of sound that reflect regional or local dialects and must modify her or his teaching strategy either to agree with these pronunciations or to accept them as equally correct as those provided in class materials and used perhaps by only a portion of the class. In some dialects, for example, the final *d* in *band, hand,* and *stand* is often not pronounced. If the teacher asks the students for other words ending in /d/, pupils may respond with /ban/, /ham/, or /stan/, which, in such circumstances, is correct. If uncertainty exists, asking the child to use the word in a sentence will demonstrate whether the word supplied is correctly used though pronounced differently from what is being sought. Such correct responses do not interfere with decoding since the dialect variation reflects the appropriate meaning. The teacher should recall that all dialect differences are correct pronunciations and should defer to those pronunciations in teaching reading. Arbitrary standards have no relevance in teaching decoding. The teacher should keep this in mind if he or she changes the pronunciation given in a phonics text or material to the pronunciation dominant in or characteristic of an area.

Consonant clusters can be presented using the activities shown for regular consonants. Note that the sounds represented by each letter in the clusters *bl, cl, pl, str, tr, br, cr, dr, fl, gr, pr, sp, st, mp,* and *nd* are pronounced as any one cluster is introduced. The clusters *mp* and *nd* do not appear in initial positions; *sp* and *st* may appear in either initial or final positions. *Camp, damp, dump, jump, lamp, limp, lump, and, band, bend, end, find, round,* and *send* may be used for the clusters *mp* and *nd; stamp, stump, stand,* for *st, mp* and *nd; star, start, step, stick, stop, store, best, chest, cost, crust, dust, fast, first, last, most, must, rest, spark, speed, spell, spill, spin, spoon, spot, crisp, grasp,* for *st* and *sp.*

However, when children have developed clear-cut associations of symbol with sound, they are capable of decoding any of the clusters and merely need to use their skill in blending the sequence of sounds represented by letters to produce particular words. Although it is often recommended that the clusters given above be taught, the decoding program may also exclude cluster recognition with no negative effects. The only apparent benefit of teaching clusters seems to be to help some children overcome the tendency to continue to "sound out" each letter to decode a word, rather than moving to a procedure that uses the rapid pronunciation of larger units. Since blending procedures recommend grouping vowel-consonant and consonant-vowel combinations, the above activity is often repetitive or pointless.

Regular Consonant Digraphs

Clusters, as illustrated and defined above, refer to two or three letters, each of which represents a distinct phoneme. *Consonant digraphs* refer to those two-letter consonant clusters that represent one sound, and that sound is usually different than the sounds represented by either letter: *ph* represents /f/; *gh,* /f/ or /g/; *ch,* /ch/, /ʃh/, or /k/; *th,* /th/ or /th/; *sh,* /ʃh/; *wh,* /h/ or /hw/. Only *ph* and *sh* can be considered *regular* consonant digraphs since each consistently represents only one sound. The use of the word *usually* in the last part of the definition of a consonant digraph is meaningful since *s* represents the /ʃh/ sound in *sure* and *sugar*—the same sound that *sh* represents in *ship*—and the *c* of *ch* represents the digraph sound in *cello.* Only *p* and *t* in the digraphs *ph* and *th* never represent the sound associated with those digraphs. Note also that this adds a third usage of the term *digraph.* It was used earlier to describe merely two letters; to refer to the glided sounds /oi/ and /ou/, neither of which is represented by one letter; and, as above, to indicate a very limited number of two-letter consonant sequences that represent one sound not usually associated with either letter. These differences can be distinguished in instruction by referring to *vowel* digraphs or to *consonant* digraphs, but the terms *spelling patterns* or *graphemes* can also be used to call attention to spelling patterns of high frequency, eliminating any need for the child to learn another term.

Procedures for teaching the regular consonant digraphs *ph* and *sh* are identical to those for regular consonant letters. Words such as *ship, shore, shelf, shop, shot, short, bush, brush, dish, dash, crash, fish, fresh, rush, wish, finish, phone, phonograph, telegraph,* and *physical,* and names such as *Philip, Joseph,* and *Philadelphia,* can be used for association activities. The recognition that a group of words all begin and end with the same two letters *and* with the same sound can be reinforced by indicating that together the two letters stand for one sound. Reference to the function of the diacritic *h* can also be made by indicating that when a letter such as *p* or *s* is followed by *h,* "the *h* is silent but acts as a signal to tell us that the *p* or *s* represents a different sound from what we usually expect."

A comparison of *s* plus *ip,* as in *sip, h* plus *ip,* as in *hip,* and *s* plus *h* plus *ip, ship,* can be used to illustrate that separately the *s* and *h* represent their own sounds but that together they represent /ʃh/; or that *s* plus *ip* equals *sip,* but when *h* comes after *s* the *s* always is pronounced /ʃh/. Since *s* in *sugar* and *sure* represents /ʃh/, reference to *h* as a signal in all other words will help in teaching the child that letters can represent more than one sound, will promote the establishment of a set for diversity, and will assist in recall and use of generalizations of high utility.

Irregular Consonant Letters and Digraphs

As has been demonstrated in Chapter 2, few consonant letters represent only one sound: *s* is pronounced /s/, /z/, /ʃh/, and /ʒ/; *c* is pronounced /k/, /s/, and occasionally /ʃh/ and /ʤh/; *ch* is pronounced /k/, /ʃh/, and /tʃh/ (but both contained in the symbol /ʤh/); *th* is pronounced /ᵗh/ and /ᵈh/; and so on. The work of Levin (1963), Williams (1968), and Chapman (1971) suggests that variable correspondences such as those above should be introduced concurrently. For example, Levin found that when at the outset of experiments children learned that graphemes represented more than one sound, they developed an expectation, or set for diversity, that was of value in transfer to decoding other words. In similar experiments, Gibson, an associate of Levin, reported that if a set for diversity was not established, difficulty in making a transfer to decoding new words occurred. Thus, if the child learned that *a* represents both /a/ and

/u/, or that *s* represents /s/ and /z/, he or she was found to more accurately decode new words containing that letter. Although there is no evidence to suggest that a slight delay in teaching the variable correspondences has negative effects, it is important that a mind set for diversity be established from the onset of instruction and that the *major alternative pronunciations* be given attention in initial activities. It is important to emphasize major alternative pronunciations in instruction since the attempt to teach all the phonemes a symbol can represent serves only to confuse children. Thus, first-day activities might begin with the correspondences *a* represents /a/; *n*, /n/; and *t*, /t/. The culmination should be activities in which pupils see that they are on the road to reading and writing, the motivation with which they enter school. Additional activities should show that when *a* is used as a word, it represents the sound /u/ as in the phrase *a tan ant*, as previously described.

Directed instruction following the frequency sound-order procedure does not preclude teaching variable correspondences concurrently. The latter is merely a suggested sequence to ensure that correspondences between symbols and the sounds of speech are developed. Decoding should be developed as rapidly as possible so that the child behaves independently when confronted with words. In teaching the correspondence between consonant letters and digraphs that represent more than one sound, the generalized techniques as illustrated above can be modified as follows:

1. Place on a pocket chart, table, or chalkboard, two words beginning with *c* and two words ending with *s*. In one of the words in which *c* appears, it represents /s/, and in the other word, /k/; in one of the words in which *s* appears, it represents /s/, and in the other word, /z/: *city-can, yes-has*. Pronounce the words and ask the children to note that both words in each pair begin or end with the same letter, but that the letter represents different beginning or ending sounds.

2. Pronounce and place other words in columns so that the words are classified by sound. Words might also be supplied by class members or, preferably, the teacher and added to the lists; for example,

> *c* as /k/: *cabin, camel, can, cap, car, cash, curve, color, corn, cup*
> *c* as /s/: *cent, circle, certain, city, center, cement*
> *s* as /s/: *bus, circus, gas, us, yes*
> *s* as /z/: *as, does, goes, has, hers, his, is, was, birds, buds, hugs*

3. Help the children to recognize that *c* represents both /k/ and /s/ by using additional words in a game-type activity where each child is supplied two cards of different colors, one of which represents *c* when pronounced as /k/ and the other *c* when pronounced as /s/. In random order, pronounce words in which the sound /k/ or /s/ is in the initial, final, or medial position. Ask the children to hold up the appropriate card to show that they know which sound — /k/ or /s/ — is being represented. The same procedure would be followed for *s* or any other letter.

4. Introduce the generalization that "*c* before *e, i,* and *y* usually represents /s/" to encourage sensitivity to its use. Some children may begin to discover this generalization on their own at this time. In either case, whether this generalization is new to them or whether they have recognized it on their own, additional words should be provided so as to reinforce its use and to reduce uncertainty in determining the sound that *c* represents. Other activities might include using two lists of words grouped according to pronunciation of *c* and visible on the board or in the pocket chart; and displaying a series of additional words containing the letter *c* and asking the class members to tell to which list each new word belongs. Children will demonstrate their understanding of the generalization when asked to verbalize why they think a word belongs with a particular list. In any case, the child's responses should be confirmed or denied by pronouncing the word.

5. The same steps used with *c* and *s* may be used with the consonant *g* in initial positions, though information on the generalization "*g* before *e, i,* or *y* usually represents /j/" might be deferred until pupils have a larger vocabulary store. Some words of value in instruction include: *gas, get, go, gift, girl, give, got, giant, general, gem, gentle,* and perhaps *gigantic.* The major variant sounds of *x,* /ks/ and /gz/, might be taught using such words as *expect, taxi, Texas, fox, fix, exact, examine,* and *example.*

Words containing the variant sounds in medial positions may also be used in this procedure, avoiding where possible the sound /sh/ as represented by *c* or *s* before *i* in initial activities. The teacher should be aware that dialect pronunciations in certain locales may not always distinguish *s* as /z/ and should temper instruction on the variant sounds of *s* by reference to local norms.

Irregular consonant digraphs such as *th, wh, ch,* and *gh* may be introduced in a similar fashion. In each case begin by using illustrative words such as *them-thing, tooth-smooth, chair-Christmas, church-stomach, what-who,* and *ghost-laugh,* which contain the major alternative pronunciations. The addition of information such as *ch* always represents /k/ before another consonant or that *wh* is only pronounced /h/ before *o* may be added after a series of words are presented.

Vowel Graphemes

As demonstrated in Chapter 4, vowel graphemes represent a variety of phonemes. The procedures suggested above for use with regular consonant letters, clusters, and digraphs are ordinarily valuable in developing the association of any one vowel letter with the most frequent sound it represents when a frequency sound-order procedure is followed. Additional procedures in teaching vowel letter correspondences also include the procedures suggested for irregular consonant letters and digraphs, the use of grapheme bases and the use of generalizations having high utility.

The following sequence, using /a/, *apple,* as an example, illustrates a variety of activities that can be used to promote the association of symbol with sound in teaching vowel grapheme-phoneme correspondences didactically.

1. Display the key-word card *apple* and ask children to tell what the object is. Point out that the /a/ sound is called an unglided (or short) vowel sound.

2. Use auditory perception activities, as suggested earlier for consonants, to help children search for, recognize, and discriminate the sound in a variety of word contexts. Have children listen first to successive words containing the sound; then have them listen to pairs of words, only one of which contains the sound, and ask which word contains the /a/ sound. To ensure attention to the task, vary the activity so that sometimes both words contain the same vowel sound. Use the terms *unglided vowel* or *short sound* /a/ whenever the opportunity arises. Ask the question, "Which word contains the unglided or short sound of /a/: *cat* or *came, bat* or *bet, sat* or *fat?*" Ask children to supply other words containing the /a/ sound and list these on the board.

3. Call attention to the letter *a,* which represents the sound /a/, and note that the letter also represents other sounds that will be learned later. Have children underline the letter in words printed on the board, repeating the sound that the letter represents.

4. Using duplicated material that contains pictures of objects labeled with their names, all of which contain the letter *a* representing the /a/ sound, ask children to say the word the object represents and to find and underline the letter that represents the unglided or short vowel sound /a/.

5. Use similar pictures of objects whose names do and do not include the unglided /a/, and repeat the underlining activity noted above.

6. A more difficult exercise, similar to the one described in steps 4 and 5, would be to include some pictures with names that contain another sound for the letter *a*, such as *ball, rain,* and *automobile.*

7. When letters such as *n* and *t* are learned in succeeding sessions, demonstrate that the letter *a* plus *n* represents the word *an; a* plus *t* represents the word *at;* and so on.

8. If writing of the letters is also provided for, exercises consisting of writing the letter *a* in blank spaces in words that are labels for pictures of objects can be developed.

9. Repetitive activity must be structured to ensure the development of the association of sound with symbol. When two or more unglided vowel sounds have been taught, reference to the partial rule "vowel letters followed by one or two consonants usually represent an unglided vowel sound" can be made. Since /a/ and /ɑ/ (as well as /u/) are unglided vowel sounds, the use of contrastive procedures described for irregular consonants should be utilized to help children determine that the /ɑ/ sound is usually found before *r* and in such words as *father.*

Grapheme Bases

The term *grapheme* has been used to refer to individual letters as well as to digraphs that represent one sound. Such recurring patterns as *at, et, it, an, en, in, un, ad, ed, id, od, ud, ap, ip, op, up, ag, eg, ig, og, ug, ack, eck, ick, ock, uck, ild, old, igh, ind, all, ell,* and *ill* can also be called graphemes; however, this would make the meaning of the term unnecessarily wide. Instead, the construct *grapheme base* is utilized to refer to these patterns and continues the reference to the graphemes of which they are composed. *Grapheme bases* are two- and three-letter units that recur in a series of words in which only the initial consonant or consonant cluster differ. A number of such grapheme bases can be learned and decoded as units because they recur frequently. The ability to recognize and use such units aids the child in decoding because graphemic bases are largely consistent in sound correspondence. Skailand's research (1970) confirmed this when she found, working with kindergarten children of low socioeconomic background, that the mean scores on a recall of words and syllables were almost twice as high for pupils who were taught by a grapheme-base approach as for pupils who were taught by whole-word or single grapheme-phoneme approaches. It has long been recognized that third- and fourth-grade children as well as adults tend to decode using familiar units, and Gibson (1970) suggests that first-grade children also perceive and use such larger letter units.

Principles of grapheme-base instruction include searching for recurring patterns. Gibson (1970) indicated that finding a recurring pattern is immediately reinforcing and pointed out that when a child makes such a discovery, he or she is apt to repeat the discovery in other words. This then becomes a useful procedure in decoding strategy. Although Gibson's conclusion is not original (teachers for years have encouraged children to find "little words in big words" and have emphasized rhyming words so as to develop sensitivity to the use of the grapheme base), her work confirms the value others had seen in using grapheme bases. Although the words *an, at, in, up, all,* and *ill* appear in the list of grapheme bases shown above, "little word" should not be used to describe grapheme bases since it does not cover all the variant sounds that the grapheme base can represent. For example, exception to the correspondence of *at* with /at/ in *bat, sat, fat* is seen in the word *what,* where *at* represents /ot/. When such different correspondences occur, they should be noted as exceptions and the correspondence of *a* with /o/ and so on, in such words as *what,* discussed. Alternatively, sight-vocabulary procedures used with irregularly spelled words among the 180 most frequent words given in Table 17 might be used to teach the correspondence of *what* with its speech sounds.

Sat, rat, fat illustrates one of these recurring patterns in which the component graphemes fairly consistently represent the same series of phonemes. The grapheme base *ell* regularly appears in *tell, fell, well, smell,* and *spell;* and *ack,* in *tack, pack, smack,* and *crack.* Vowel graphemes in these cases also quite regularly follow the first part of the rule that states that "vowels followed by one or two consonant letters are usually unglided. . . ."

Instructional procedure for grapheme bases should continue to emphasize the principle of searching for and discovering the recurring patterns, and a mind-set should be established for the child to use this principle in his or her decoding strategy. Rhyming words can, or course, be taught directly using procedures described above. Similarly, the procedure of changing the initial consonant letter—in which, for instance, *f, t, k, w, sp, th,* and so on are alternatively substituted and added to the grapheme base *ill*—has been used to advantage in developing decoding skill. But in neither case does the procedure appear to ensure transfer to decoding strategy to the same extent as does a strategy that emphasizes thinking for first-day activity using the symbols *a, n,* and *t.* The "thinking" strategy is as follows:

1. When the symbols *a, n,* and *t* are introduced, the words *an, Nan, Nat, ant, Ann, at,* and *tan* are developed by combining single-letter associations and listed on the board. Directing the pupils' attention to the listed words, explain that "some of the words belong together because they contain the same two letters." Have the pupils identify which words belong together by underlining one set of words and circling the other. The emphasis here is on indicating that a pattern exists and on having the children identify the pattern for themselves. The activity is relatively easy since the words *an* and *at* are contained in the list. The list can be sorted again by writing each of the words that contain the recurring pattern under the heading *at* and *an.*

Since directed instruction on the use of letters to represent sounds included pronouncing the words found when, for example, *a* and *n* are selected to form the word *an,* grapheme-base correspondence with sound may already have been accomplished by some children. However, pronouncing each of the words and calling attention to the pronunciation of the bases *at* and *an* should be done to aid the class make the association of the bases with their sounds.

2. Another list of words, such as *ant, Santa, Nat, rat, bat, bit, tan, sat, Nan, net, ban,* and *tab,* in which the two recurring patterns are found but in which some exceptions occur, may be used at a later stage or even used during second-day developmental activities to provide additional practice in searching for and identifying the recurring patterns. Even though directed association between additional consonant or vowel letters and the sounds they represent has not yet been done, such words as *cat, pat, fat, mat, flat, that,* and *can, pan, fan, man, than,* can be presented and pronounced. Attention can then be called to the fact that the two letters at the end of these words all sound the same. Initial letters can be covered up to

focus attention on the recurring pattern while either pronouncing it or asking children to pronounce it.

3. When additional correspondences between consonant letters and their sounds have been taught, a series of words such as those shown in steps 1 and 2 as well as others should be listed in a column to provide transfer practice in decoding new words. The first word might be pronounced and the pupils asked to read the others: *bell, fell, tell, well, spell,* or *ball, tall, call, fall, wall.*

4. The transfer problem should next be made more complex by presenting a random order of words containing three or more recurring patterns. This is done because reading a list of rhyming words does not promote searching for and using grapheme bases in decoding new words.

5. Next list a series of words beginning with the same consonant or consonant cluster to encourage children to note the varying recurrent patterns following the initial consonant or cluster: *can, cat, cut, call, cad, cod, cud, cap, cup,* or *spell, spill, spat, spit, span, spin, spun, sped.*

The procedures described above not only focus on recognition of the recurring patterns in words but also develop or reinforce symbol-sound correspondences for vowel graphemes. With most children, repetitive practice might preclude the need to teach the use of the first part of the generalization that "vowels followed by one or two letters are usually unglided. . . ." Or, alternatively, the generalization may be derived inductively after repetitive practice. Although the use of generalizations, whether taught didactically or developed inductively as shown below, should not be avoided, correspondences such as *ca, co, cu, ce,* and *ci* in such words as *cab, car, cap, cat, cob, cop, cut, cub, cup, cent, center, cellar, city,* and *cigar* may also be taught as grapheme bases or used to reinforce the generalization that "*c* before *e, i,* and *y* usually represents /s/." When the grapheme-base concept is taught, additional reinforcement of the quality of the vowel following *c* is developed, and the extension of the concept that we must use the letters following *c* to help determine which sound the letter *c* represents is provided for.

Correspondences Using Contrasting Spelling Patterns

Contrasting spelling patterns, as seen in the words *can-cane, rod-rode, cut-cute, met-mete, dine-dinner, rod-road, pad-paid, met-meet, net-neat, he-her,* and *no-not,* can be used to introduce the major alternative correspondences of symbol with sound; to demonstrate the function of the diacritic *e;* to reinforce the use of unglided sounds signaled when followed by one or two consonant letters; or to show the function of a following vowel in such words as *meet, goat,* or *laid.*

The function of the diacritic *e* is by far the most important of the rules to be taught. It can be developed by using parallel columns showing the alternation from the unglided to the glided sound by using the *e: rat-rate, can-cane, cap-cape, hat-hate, mad-made, pal-pale, tap-tape,* and so on. A more desirable initial procedure is to use in random order a series of words containing different vowels representing the unglided and glided sounds. It should be explained that the words can be separated into two different groups, and the children should be asked to tell which words belong together. Often, the prompt that pupils should look at the end of the words is necessary. Searching for and discovering the pattern is desired; thus, initially, no reference to the final *e* should be made.

After the words are sorted, arrange them in pairs, pronounce the words in each pair, and ask the children if the words sound the same. Point out that the words in each pair are written differently as well; namely, that one word has another letter. Children might also be asked to indicate this difference. Continue through the lists of words, and then point out that vowel letters can represent more than one sound and that the *e* at the end of many words acts as a signal to indicate that the preceding vowel letter represents the glided sound. Do not suggest "that the *e makes* the preceding vowel say its own name," since that is not the case. As we know, letters can represent glided and unglided sounds in the absence of *e,* and letters do not say anything. The function of the final *e* is only as a signal of the quality of the vowel letter and in itself has no sound value.

Additional pairs of words in repetitive exercises should be used to develop and fix this concept. Practice in recognition of the function of the diacritic *e* in relation to one vowel letter at a time should follow next. For example, write *at* and *ate* on the board; ask the pupils how they would be pronounced; then add consonant letters such as *p, m, r,* and *s* to each to form the words *pat-pate, mat-mate, rat-rate, sat-sate,* to achieve further recognition of the function of the diacritic *e.*

Using such pairs of words as *pad-paid, lad-laid,* and *mad-maid,* listed in random order, procedures should be followed to note the function of the second vowel in each instance. Additional pairs such as *cot-coat*, *got-goat*, *red-read*, *bled-bleed*, *red-reed*, and *bet-beet* should then be introduced. The generalization that "*ai*, *ay*, *oa*, and *ee* usually represent the glided sound of the first vowel" can be stated, or the generalization that "some vowels when followed by another letter usually represent the glided sound of the first vowel" can be recognized. Exceptions to the rules such as *said-says* should be noted.

Patterns such as *he-hem*, *me-men*, *no-not*, *go-got*, *dine-dinner*, *wine-winner*, *ripe-ripped*, and *ride-ridden* can be introduced in a similar fashion, pointing out that vowels at the end of short words usually represent the glided sound of the vowel (except *a*, which represents one of the unglided sounds of *a*), and that vowels followed by one or two consonant letters are usually unglided. When exceptions occur, the use of procedures as suggested for irregular consonant letters and digraphs and the development of a set for diversity are recommended. Transfer practice to additional word groups must be used consistently to effect the development of appropriate decoding strategy.

Correspondences Using Generalizations

As noted for the irregular consonants, for consonants followed by *h*, and for vowel sounds signaled by the diacritic *e*, the generalization that applies to any set of consistent correspondences can be stated first. It should then be followed by a display of words to which that generalization applies and practice in searching for and applying the generalization in additional words. An alternative procedure can be followed: list a series of words; encourage children to sort them by contrasting the spelling patterns; and then supply the generalization that applies or encourage children to state the generalization in their own words. This procedure is of value in establishing the set to search for familiar patterns or similar spellings that agree with the generalization. It is more desirable to use the first procedure of stating the generalization since many instances exist where confusion over patterns can arise. The *e* following *v* or *z* to indicate that the *v* or *z* is never word-final, for example, needs to be taught not only to ensure that the diacritic *e* for vowels once removed in vowel-consonant-plus *e* patterns will have a high practical utility but also to avoid confusion in such words as *give, live,* and *have.*

Sight-Word Recognition

Since efficient and effective reading at the earliest point possible is dependent upon the child's ability to recognize certain words at a glance, and since some words cannot be decoded either by using correspondences developed in phonics instruction or by generalizations, a number of words must be taught as sight words. The generalized procedure below emphasizes the principles that words should be used in oral contexts first, and that sight words are developed using a meaningful sentence context.

1. Before showing children a new sight word, use it orally in various meaningful contexts. Children should recognize the word as one in their oral vocabulary before they see it written. To make certain that they have identified the word as one in their oral vocabulary, ask them to use it in a sentence. For example, "Do you know what the word *give* means?" Or, "Can you use the word *the* in a sentence?"

2. The first written presentation of a sight word should be in a meaningful sentence context. Write a sentence on the board, underlining the sight word as you pronounce it. (In presenting the printed form of a new word, always make sure that the children are actually looking at the new word as you pronounce it.) After examining the word in the sentence, ask pupils to pronounce it and discuss its meaning or function in the sentence. The example for *the* is illustrated. *The,* frequently used and frequently troublesome, is difficult to define and is best demonstrated by its inclusion or omission in sentences. The determiner *the,* seen over and over again by the beginner, is a natural part of speech. Demonstrate its use by writing on the board a sentence such as "The dog ran into the street." Read the sentence orally, omitting the articles to help children recognize the awkwardness of the incomplete construction. The teacher should note, however, that the sentence "Dog ran into street" may also be viewed as perfectly correct since the article *the* is often eliminated in some dialects. In such cases, the teacher should point out that sometimes people speak without using the word *the* but that it will always be used in the books they are to read.

3. The procedure of presenting sight words can be extended to include some of the following activities.

a. Have children examine the visual characteristics of a sight word, such as its length, shape, and ascending and descending characters *(b, d, p, g, y, j)* of the letters in it. Such visual clues, as noted earlier, help children recognize new words and discriminate between words of similar configuration.

b. Provide opportunities for children to match words and phrases on cards with the words and phrases in experience stories they have been writing or participating in the development of. Call on children to find, frame, and read words in sentences on the chalkboard or on charts. Help children to recognize that words in books are the same as those they learned to read from the chalkboard and experience charts by asking them to search for and then underline or circle such words in duplicated printed story materials.

c. Have children identify new letters in words by presenting the letters of a word one at a time in a pocket chart using letter cards. Without teaching new letters or new patterns, simply supply the corresponding sound and give the key word for the sound. It's possible that some children may even be able to figure out the pronunciation of the word by themselves when a number of letters are shown.

The accompanying list of "sight words" (Table 17), identified as the most frequently used words in print, can be developed sequentially as the decoding program unfolds; developed as the words appear in experience stories or printed materials; or even developed as a game in which children who have learned to respond to a rapid presentation of each word in a short space of time are rewarded by recognition as members of the "Sight-Word Club." The list is modified from that known as the Dolch list of 220 words by recent research of Hillerich (1974), Johns (1975), and others who have found certain words in the original list as being less frequently used.

The words *the, of, and, to, a, in, that, it, is,* and *I,* according to the research of Dewey (1923), constitute 25 percent of the total number of running words in any page of discourse. These ten words would obviously be of high value in learning to read since they are used so frequently. The early date of Dewey's research may suggest to some that rather antique findings are being indicated for use in modern instructional programs. Recent research, however, has generally supported these early findings and differs from them

TABLE 17. The Basic Sight-Word Vocabulary in American English

a	done	I	only
about	don't	if	open
after	down	in	or
again	draw	into	our
all		is	out
always	eat	it	over
am	every	its	own
an			
and	fall	just	play
any	far		pretty
are	fast	keep	pull
around	find	kind	put
as	first	knew	
ask	five		ran
at	for	let	read
away	found	light	red
	four	like	right
be	from	little	round
because	full	live	run
been		long	
before	gave	look	said
best	get		saw
better	give	made	say
big	go	make	see
black	goes	many	shall
blue	going	may	she
both	good	me	show
bring	got	much	six
but	green	must	small
buy	grow	my	so
by		myself	some
	had		soon
call	has	never	start
came	have	new	stop
can	he	no	
carry	help	not	take
cold	her	now	tell
come	here		ten
could	him	of	thank
cut	his	off	that
	hold	old	the
did	hot	on	their
do	how	once	them
does	hurt	one	then

TABLE 17. The Basic Sight-Word Vocabulary in American English (Continued)

there	two	warm	why
these		was	will
they	under	we	wish
think	up	well	with
this	upon	went	work
those	us	were	would
three	use	what	write
to		when	
today	very	where	
together		which	yes
too	walk	white	you
try	want	who	your

principally because different materials were used to develop a corpus of words. For example, the words *the, a, to, and, of, in, you, is, he,* and *it* were found to have the highest frequency by Otto and Chester (1972). They, in turn, compared their findings with the rankings of Dolch (1941), Kučera and Francis (1967), and Johnson (1971). Otto and Chester felt that the first ten words of these latter studies were in close agreement with each other but criticized the studies as being based on samples of words that were not directly related to instructional materials. They pointed out that *you,* which appeared as the seventh most frequent word in their study, was ranked thirty-third in the others.

Moe (1973), developed a frequency listing based on a study of the vocabulary found in trade books for young children. His findings show some similarity to those of Dewey as well as to those of Otto and Chester. The lack of agreement that is shown is based on the different samples of materials used. Yet almost all studies follow-ing Dewey agree with his findings that *the, of, and, to,* and *a* are ranked from highest to lowest in frequency.

Dewey's findings indicate that the first sixty-nine words of highest frequency *(the, of, and, to, a, in, that, it, is, I, for, he, was, as, you, with, he, on, have, by, not, at, this, are, we, his, but, they, all, or, which, will, from, had, has, one, our, an, been, no, their, there, were, so, my, if, me, what, would, who, when, him, them, her, your, any, more, now, its, time, up, do, out, can, than, only, she, made, into)* comprise 50 percent of running words in discourse. Again, these sixty-nine would be of greatest significance for teaching in a sight-vocabulary program.

Note that the sight words *a, it, in, and,* and many of the others can also be decoded on a grapheme-phoneme correspondence basis, and that flash-card exercises can be used so that they can be recognized in .04 seconds or less. Alternative procedures are *always* available in instructional strategy and should be utilized rather than fixing on one approach.

Phonics, Blending Difficulties, and Auditory Closure

Horace Mann advocated the word method and ridiculed the spelling procedure for word learning found in Webster's *Spelling Book;* he characterized it as the "see-a-tee-cat, pee-you-tee-put, tee-aitch-ee-the school of thought." The later phonic methods (often called phonetic) of Leigh and Isaac Pitman were spelling methods as well, but in these methods words were spelled by their elementary sounds and not by letter names. The word was slowly pronounced until the child became aware of its constituent sounds. Drill in this kind of sound analysis trains articulation and the ear, but it should also develop the child's ability to pronounce a word by blending the sounds. Associating sounds already known with the symbols of the alphabet used to represent them, however, often proceeds using a different rationale. If the letters *a* and *t* are isolated, the first associated with the beginning sound in the word *apple,* the second with the beginning sound in *table,* and the child is asked to pronounce the word meant, he or she may exhibit difficulty in blending the sounds to produce the word *at.* The problem, as discovered early in the use of alphabetic or phonetic approaches, was also found to exist when children were instructed using intrinsic phonic approaches found in basal readers. Chall (1967:351) noted that

> *The Carden Method* and *The Writing Road to Reading* teach the child to blend words orally and then visually. Most other systems tend to skirt blending. In fact, they discourage it for fear that extraneous sounds will be introduced or, as Fries and Bloomfield contend, that the sounds corresponding to individual letters are not consistent and serve only to confuse the child.

Bishop's (1964) and Levin's (1963) studies, however, provide evidence to suggest that Bloomfield and Fries were in error.

There is no distortion of sound when the continuants (sounds that may be prolonged without change in quality) /m/ and /n/ are separated or used in combination with a vowel phoneme: /m/ can be stretched out so long as air holds out, with no reason ever to say /muh/. Similarly, the phones in the final positions of words such as *ti*[p] and *ta*[b] can be pronounced without distortion, unless we assume the phones [p] and [b] in the final position of words are already distorted.

Research has indicated that the ability to blend sounds to form words is not related to chronological or mental age, though bright children often develop the ability earlier than others. Chall et al. (1963:116) note that "auditory blending ability whether tested in the first grade, second, third, or fourth grades is positively correlated with oral and silent reading ability through the fourth grade," and that auditory blending is a significant factor in beginning reading.

Coleman (1972) demonstrated that procedures used in helping children to blend should emphasize the use of vowel plus consonant *(u-p, o-t, i-t)* patterns first, and that exercise in these should be followed by consonant plus vowel patterns *(t-oo)*. He demonstrated, too, that the vowel and consonant letters might ordinarily be utilized in a given sequence and reported that vowel-consonant syllables beginning with glided vowels and ending with such consonants as *t* or *f* were significantly easier to learn than those syllables that began with an unglided vowel and ended with these same consonants.

Table 18 has been organized to present the sequence of learnability of the consonant and vowel phonemes when presented in vowel-consonant or consonant-vowel syllables. This table allows the reader to generate hundreds of two-sound syllables to help children grasp the blending concept. It provides material for daily game type exercises lasting a few minutes each. The first glided vowel phoneme could be paired with each of the consonant phonemes listed to create both nonsense and meaningful syllables; this could be followed by pairing the second glided vowel phoneme with each of the consonants; and so on. On the other hand, a decision could be made to use only those vowel-consonant syllables that represent words or elements in words, eliminating nonsense syllables. In any case, based on the needs of children in a given class, the various syllables could be extended using the procedure that follows.

Using the vowel phoneme /ou/ and the consonant phoneme /t/ in the vowel-consonant-syllable section of the table, for example, say to the children, "I'm going to say two sounds that are found in

TABLE 18. Ease of Learning Sequence for Vowel-Consonant and Consonant-Vowel Syllables

Vowel-Consonant Syllables		Consonant-Vowel Syllables	
Vowel Phoneme	Consonant Phoneme	Consonant Phoneme	Vowel Phoneme
/oi/	/t/	/z/	/æ/
/ou/	/th/	/b/	/oi/
/ue/	/ʃh/	/f/	/ie/
/o/	/f/	/v/	/œ/
/ie/	/ch/	/m/	/ɛɛ/
/ɛɛ/	/p/	/k/	/ω/
/au/	/z/	/p/	/ou/
/æ/	/g/	/ʃh/	/au/
/œ/	/h/	/t/	/o/
/ω/	/k/	/ch/	/a/
/e/	/v/	/g/	/ur/
/u/	/j/	/d/	/ue/
/ur/	/r/	/s/	/e/
/a/	/d/	/h/	/i/
/i/	/m/	/r/	
	/n/	/j/	
	/l/	/th/	
		/n/	
		/w/	
		/wh/	
		/l/	

the word which is the opposite of *in*. See if you can tell me what word I'm saying." Say /ou/, pause, and then say /t/. Repeat the phonemes once more to see if any children can say the word. If you receive no response, repeat the sounds and say the word *out*. Repeat the exercise with /oi/ and /l/, /ɛɛ/ and /t/, /ɛɛ/ and /ch/, /ɛɛ/ and /r/, /ɛɛ/ and /l/, /o/ and /n/, /ie/ and /d/, /ie/ and /m/, /ie/ and /l/.

The procedure used here is to select a vowel phoneme that in combination with a consonant phoneme represents a meaningful word. It starts with the easiest to learn and moves to the more difficult. The procedure can be extended as needed to such syllables as /oi/ and /t/ and /oi/ and /n/, since they represent syllables found in words such as *quoits* and *coin*.

The teaching of blending, or auditory closure as it is often referred to, is a basic step in the development of decoding skills. Once you have helped children through the process of associating letters with sounds they represent you may still find that some of the slower-learning children earnestly attempt to "sound out" a word yet do not arrive at the actual word. Such children do not seem to grasp the process of synthesizing elements into a meaningful whole. In order to help such children to develop skill in this crucial process the procedure below may be followed.

Say to the children, "I'm going to say a name sound by sound. See if you can tell which name I'm saying." Repeat the procedure with several names, sometimes sounding the names out sound by sound (as in *B-e-n*), sometimes separating the elements in the consonant-vowel-consonant pattern /b—en/ or /be—n/.

As a variation and progression of this activity, say to the children, "Now I'm thinking about something in this room. I will say its name with separate sounds [e.g., /d-e-s-k/, /cœ-t/, /d-or/]. Try to put the sounds together to make the name I am thinking of." (Use the same variety of approaches to separating elements described above.)

A further step in this activity would be to use words that are common in the child's vocabulary. Words that are introduced in experience stories should be used in this activity, for instance, *b-o-x, h-ouse, d-oll*.

Care should be taken that this activity is not overdone. Daily sessions of five to six minutes are appropriate.

If the child is having difficulty, place the word that is broken up into the context of a sentence. For example, a teacher might say, "Please close the *d—oor*." Even if the children are proceeding smoothly through the auditory closure training sessions, it is wise to include some practice in grasping broken-up words in sentence contexts. This point is emphasized because, if the children learn this skill well, they will apply it as a word-attack approach in their actual reading.

REFERENCES

Anderson, Roger A., and Samuels, S. Jay. "Visual Recognition Memory, Paired Associate Learning, and Reading Achievement." Paper presented at AERA Convention, Minneapolis, March 1970.

Bailey, Mildred Hart. "The Utility of Phonic Generalizations in Grades One Through Six." *The Reading Teacher* 20 (1967): 413 – 418.

Bishop, C. N. "Transfer Effects of Word and Letter Training in Reading." *Journal of Verbal Learning and Verbal Behavior* 3 (1964): 215 – 221.

Black, Elsie D. "A Study of Consonant Situations in a Primary Reading Vocabulary." Master's thesis, Temple University, 1950.

Black, Sister Mary Carlo, B.V.M. "Phonic Rules Verification by a Thirteen Hundred Word Count." Master's project, Loyola University of Los Angeles, 1961.

Black, Millard. "A Study of Certain Structural Elements of Words in a Primary Reading Vocabulary." Master's thesis, Temple University, 1950.

Bleismer, Emery P., and Yarborough, Betty H. "A Comparison of Ten Different Beginning Reading Programs in First Grade." *Phi Delta Kappan* 46 (1965): 500 – 504.

Burmeister, Lou E. "Word Analysis-Corrective Reading in the Secondary School." *Journal of the Reading Specialist* 5 (1968): 100 – 104.

Chall, Jeanne. *Learning to Read: The Great Debate.* New York: McGraw-Hill, 1967.

Chall, Jeanne, Roswell, Florence G., and Blumenthal, Susan Hahn. "Auditory Blending Ability: A Factor in Success in Beginning Reading." *The Reading Teacher* 17 (1963): 113 – 118.

Chapman, Robin S. "Use of Simple and Conditional Letter-Sound Correspondences in Children's Pronunciations of Synthetic Words." Paper presented at AERA Convention, Minneapolis, March 1971.

Clymer, Theodore L. "The Utility of Phonic Generalizations in the Primary Grades." *The Reading Teacher* 16 (1963): 252 – 258.

Coleman, Edmund. "Data Base for a Reading Technology." Monograph, *Journal of Educational Psychology,* 1972.

Cordts, Anna D. "Analysis and Classification of the Sounds of English Words in the Primary Reading Vocabulary." Ph.D. dissertation, University of Iowa, 1925.

Dewey, Godfrey. *Relative Frequency of English-Speech Sounds.* Cambridge, Mass.: Harvard University Press, 1923.

Dolch, Edward W. *Teaching Primary Reading.* Champaign, Ill.: Garrard Press, 1941.

Emans, Robert. "The Usefulness of Phonic Generalizations Above the Primary Grades." *The Reading Teacher* 20 (1967): 419 – 425.

Fry, Edward. "A Frequency Approach to Phonics." *Elementary English* 41 (1964): 759 – 765.

Gibson, Eleanor J. "Experiments on Four Aspects of Reading Skill and Its Attainment." *Project Literacy Reports,* No. 5 (1965): 1 – 12.

——— "The Ontogeny of Reading." *American Psychologist* 25 (1970): 136 – 143.

Gibson, Eleanor J., et al. "An Analysis of Critical Features of Letters Tested by a Confusion Matrix." In *A Basic Research Program on Reading,* Cornell University and U.S. Office of Education, Cooperative Research Project No. 639. Ithaca, N.Y.: Cornell University, 1963.

Hillerich, Robert L. "Word Lists — Getting It All Together." *The Reading Teacher* 26 (January 1974): 353 – 361.

Jeffrey, W. E., and Samuels, S. Jay. "The Effect of Method of Reading on Initial Reading and Transfer." *Journal of Verbal Learning and Verbal Behavior* 6 (1967): 354 – 358.

Johns, Jerry L. "The Dolch Words." *NJEA Review* 47 (March 1975): 12.

Johnson, Dale D. "The Dolch List Re-examined." *The Reading Teacher* 24 (1971): 449 – 457.

Kottmeyer, W. A. *Phonetic and Structural Generalization for the Teaching of a Primary Grade Spelling Vocabulary.* Reported in Webster Publishing Co., Reserve File No. 528-S and 529-S, St. Louis, Mo., 1954.

Kučera, Henry, and Francis, W. Nelson. *Computational Analysis of Present Day American English.* Providence: Brown University Press, 1967.

Levin, Harry. *A Basic Research Program on Reading,* Cornell University and U.S. Office of Education, Cooperative Research Project No. 639, Ithaca, N.Y.: Cornell University, 1963.

Levin, Harry, and Watson, J. "The Learning of Variable Grapheme-to-Phoneme Correspondences." *A Basic Research Program on Reading,* Final Report, Cornell University and U.S. Office of Education, Cooperative Research Project No. 639, Ithaca, N.Y.: Cornell University, 1963.

Lott, Deborah. "Visual Recognition: Its Implications for Reading Research and Instruction." Inglewood, Cal.: Southwest Regional Laboratory, 1969.

Marchbanks, C., and Levin, N. "Cues by Which Children Recognize Words." *Journal of Educational Psychology* 56 (1965): 57 – 61.

Mazurkiewicz, Albert J. *The Initial Teaching Alphabet in Reading Instruction: Evaluation-Demonstration Project on the Use of i.t.a. – Comprehensive Final Report.* Bethlehem, Pa.: Lehigh University, 1967.

–––––– "The Silent *e* Speaks Up!" *Reading World* 13 (May 1974a): 254 – 257.

–––––– "The Diacritic *e.*" *Reading World* 14 (October 1974b): 9 – 21.

–––––– "Applicability of Diacritic *e* Generalization." *Reading World* 14 (December 1974c): 104 – 111.

–––––– "What Do Teachers Know About Phonics." *Reading World* 14 (March 1975a): 165 – 177.

–––––– "What College Teachers Know About Phonics?" Paper presented at College Reading Association Convention, Bethesda, Md., October 31, 1975b.

Moe, Alden J. "Vocabularies for Beginning Readers: A Computer-Assisted Analysis of Trade Books for Young Children." Paper presented at convention of International Reading Association, Denver, May 2, 1973.

Moore, James T., Jr. "Phonetic Elements Appearing in a Three Thousand Word Spelling Vocabulary." Ph.D. dissertation, Stanford University, School of Education, 1951.

Muehl, Seigman, and King, Ethel. "A Recent Research in Visual Discrimination: Significance for Beginning Reading." In *Vistas in Reading,* International Reading Association Convention Proceedings, 1967, Part 1, 434 – 439.

Oaks, Ruth E. "A Study of the Vowel Situations in a Primary Reading Vocabulary." *Education* 72 (May 1952): 1 – 14.

Otto, Wayne, and Chester, Robert. "Sight Words for Beginning Readers." *Journal of Educational Research* 65 (July, August 1972): 435 – 443.

Pick, A. D. "Improvement of Visual and Tactual Form Discrimination." *Journal of Experimental Psychology* 69 (1965): 331 – 339.

Samuels, S. Jay. "The Effects of Letter-Name Knowledge on Learning to Read." *American Educational Research Journal* 9 (1972): 65 – 74.

Samuels, S. Jay, and Williams, Joanna P. Informal remarks at American Education Research Association Convention in New Orleans, February 1973.

Schonell, F. J. *Backwardness in Basic Subjects.* 4th ed. London: Oliver and Boyd, 1948.

Skailand, Dawn B. "A Comparison of Four Language Units in Teaching Beginning Reading." Ph.D. dissertation, University of California, 1970.

160 • TEACHING ABOUT PHONICS

Stauffer, Russell G. *Teaching Reading as a Thinking Process.* New York: Harper & Row, 1969.

Thorndike, E. L., and Lorge, I. *The Teacher's Word Book of 30,000 Words.* New York: Columbia University, Teachers College Press, 1944.

Tudor-Hart, Beatrice. "An Experiment in Methodology Using a Phonetic Alphabet." *Spelling Progress Bulletin* 8 (Spring 1969): 2 – 10.

Williams, Joanna P. "Successive vs. Concurrent Presentation of Multiple Grapheme-Phoneme Correspondences." *Journal of Educational Psychology* 59 (1968): 309 – 314.

Williams, Joanna P., Blomber, Ellen L., and Williams, David V. "Cues Used in Visual Word Recognition." *Journal of Educational Psychology* 61 (1970): 310 – 315.

Postscript

Although the basic decoding program has been characterized by difficulties in teaching grapheme-phoneme correspondences due to misinformed or inadequate research, there is no basis today for poor instructional activity in this area. Inadequate information in structural analysis has also been shown to exist. Structural analysis, usually defined as embracing compound words, "little words in big words," prefixes, roots, suffixes, syllabication, accent and dictionary, and only briefly touched on in these pages, has been denounced as misleading to children in a number of ways. However, research has been done that forms the basis for correcting such inadequacies, though it is beyond the scope of this text to deal with such research.

Spelling reform to simplify the orthography would be a commendable undertaking. This view reflects my concern not with the literate adult but with the child who must learn to read. Simplification of tasks set before the child is so obviously desirable if he or she is to avoid frustration, failure in learning, and ego damage that the issue of spelling reform must at some point be considered and acted upon. Even adults who can read experience difficulty in spelling, and in many ways that difficulty serves to further social inequality by "keeping such people in their place." Although research on the desirability, direction, and acceptance of spelling reform exists, that, too, is another area for future exploration.

Alternative approaches to simplifying the orthography for the beginner, such as Pitman's initial teaching alphabet (i.t.a.), World English Spelling, Unifon, Distar, the Goldman-Lynch Alphabet, and D.M.S. (diacritic marking system), are only hinted at here through the use of i.t.a. as a phonemic notation. A wealth of data and information on their effective use as temporary reforms of the orthography exists, although it is too vast a subject to be dealt with in a volume on phonics.

The reader is encouraged to explore these areas in the literature, but he or she is also encouraged to use the contents of this text to provide the basis for effective decoding skill so that children can become *readers* of the wealth of materials available in our rich and graceful language.

Index

ſ